THOMAS J. J. ALTIZER

THE
NEW
GOSPEL
OF
CHRISTIAN
ATHEISM

The New Gospel of Christian Atheism
©2002, Thomas J. J. Altizer

Address all requests to: The Davies Group, Publishers, PO Box 440140, Aurora, CO 80044-0140 USA

Library of Congress Cataloging-in-Publication Data

Altizer, Thomas J. J.
   The new gospel of Christian Atheism / Thomas J. J. Altizer.
   p. cm.
Rev. ed. of: The gospel of Christian Atheism.
   ISBN 1-888570-65-2
   1. Death of God theology. I. Altizer, Thomas J. J. Gospel of Christian Atheism. II. Title.
   BT83.5 .A45 2002
   231—dc21

                   2002000577

Credit is given to the Westminster Press for material originally appearing in *The Gospel of Christian Atheism* (1996).

The cover image was produced by Dr. Andrew D. Burbanks. (c.f. page xii) Cover design by The Davies Group.

Printed in the United States of America
Published 2002. The Davies Group Publishers, Aurora CO 80044-0140

1 2 3 4 5 6 7 8 9 0

For Katharine Blake Altizer

Contents

Preface

There can be little doubt that we are now entering a truly new world — the electronic technological revolution alone makes this manifest — but this new world is nevertheless a mystery to us, above all in its impact upon our interior life, and in its effect upon our deepest interior identity. Just as we can know our new world as a new exteriority, and a truly comprehensive exteriority, if that exteriority is a total exteriority it will consume our interiority itself, or threaten to do so. A new interior emptiness is increasingly real to us, an emptiness that can be understood as a consequence of our new world. This emptiness not only dominates our mass media, but is profoundly challenging both thinking and the imagination, as art itself now threatens to come to an end, or come to an end as everything that we once knew as art. At no point is this challenge more openly manifest than in our theological thinking, as a uniquely modern theological thinking is truly ending, now theology is apparently actual only as a deeply conservative or reactionary theology, and although theology is being reborn in contemporary French philosophy this is not happening elsewhere. Only a very few can now know theology as a genuine thinking that could possibly be a truly contemporary thinking. But this new crisis of theology is inseparable from a new loss of an ultimate ground, an ultimate ground that is seemingly unthinkable for us, or unthinkable as anything but an absolutely exterior ground.

Mark C. Taylor, in his preface to my theological memoir, *Living the Death of God*, identifies me as the last theologian, and perhaps I am the last modern theologian, or the last theologian who can think within the horizon of a uniquely modern world. Genuinely modern theological thinking is a fully radical theological thinking, as most openly present in our modern philosophical theologies, for until the twentieth century all of our major philosophers were theological thinkers, and Nietzsche himself could know every philosopher as being at bottom a theologian. Only in the twentieth century does a deep division arise between philosophy and theology, and while the twentieth century has known radical *philosophical* thinkers, it has known few if any radical *theological* thinkers, and seemingly none who are radical dogmatic thinkers. Many know *The Gospel of Christian Atheism* (The Westminster Press, 1966) as our most radical theological book, or our most radical "dogmatic" theology, one that attempts to discover the death of God as the very essence of the Christian faith, and to do so by unveiling a uniquely Christian crucifixion as apocalypse itself. Indeed, it is precisely apocalyptic theology that is most missing from the whole world of theology, and this despite our historical realization of the apocalyptic origin of Christianity, an origin that was profoundly transformed in the first three generations of Christian history, and an origin that has been subverted or reversed by every major post-Augustinian theology. At no other point are our multiple Christian theologies so openly united, or so deeply distant from their Biblical ground, and now Biblical scholarship and criticism are almost wholly alienated from any possible theological ground.

The absence of a theological ground is the absence of the possibility of thinking about faith, and while many embrace a pure pietism foreclosing all possibility of such thinking, just as our churches are now more distant from theology than they have ever previously been, the inevitable consequence is a radical isolation of faith from the world, and above all an isolation of faith from the actualities of our world, and religion can now seemingly be real only as a purely reactionary movement. Is there no possibility now of a theological thinking that is not a conservative or a reactionary thinking, no possibility of a radical theological thinking for us? In the face of a virtually universal judgment that only a conservative politics is now actually possible, is the advent of postmodernity the advent of the most conservative world since the ending of the Middle Ages? And has that advent ended every theology that is not a purely conservative theology, or every theology that could possibly challenge this new world? While a genuinely radical theology, *The Gospel of Christian Atheism* was very much a product of the Sixties, hence it is apparently wholly irrelevant today, but it has no counterparts at all in our world, so I accepted the task of its substantial revision in an attempt to address theologically our postmodern world. Above all, this revision is concerned to address our contemporary nihilism, one truly unique historically, and as Nietzsche knew so profoundly, a nihilism that is a consequence of Christianity, yet no real theological exploration of our nihilism now exists.

Not only is our nihilism truly new, but it could only be unreal apart from an *absolute novum*, an *absolute novum* that was first historically embodied in the birth of Christianity, and while reborn again and again in subsequent history, it only becomes comprehensively embodied in the late modern world. Hegel and Nietzsche are both primal thinkers of an *absolute novum*, and if it is Nietzsche who most purely reversed Hegel, that reversal is inseparable from the full advent of nihilism, a nihilism that is truly overwhelming in the twentieth century. Are there any genuinely imaginative expressions of our world that are not nihilistic, or any genuine thinking of ours that is not finally nihilistic? These questions have now become common questions, and they are inseparable from the advent of an absolute novum, an absolute novum that has been most profoundly explored in our world by D. G. Leahy in *Foundation: Matter the Body Itself* (SUNY, 1996). This revision is very much under the impact of Leahy, and in the concluding chapter of *Foundation* Leahy enacts a new beginning beyond both a modern and a postmodern nothingness, a modern nothingness most purely embodied in Hegelian thinking. For Leahy, Hegel's Godhead is the Nothing, the abyss of God in God, but the Hegelian absolute cannot actually die, and there is no possibility of an actual death of God in modern European thinking. Thus, the realization of the death of God occurs for the first time in history in the American consciousness, and concretely and essentially occurs in Altizer's theology, even if there it only abysmally occurs as a black mass.

Leahy has thought beyond that abyss by an essentially new thinking realizing an absolute apocalypse, and an absolute apocalypse occurring even now, and while this theologian may well have been left behind by that advent, he remains committed to a theology of the death of God, and a death of God that is itself apocalypse. Already Paul could know the crucifixion as the very advent of a final apocalypse, and if we now know that Paul's theological thinking is a purely apocalyptic thinking, it is most apocalyptic in its centering upon the crucifixion. This is the crucifixion that ever more fully becomes the center of Western Christianity, until it explodes in the Reformation, and then explodes once again in the full advent of the modern world. For in late modernity an absolute death or an absolute abyss or an absolute nothingness fully enters the imagination as it had never done so before, and if this transformation of the imagination is a fundamental ground of our nihilism, it is nevertheless a primal way to the transfiguration of our nothingness, and a transfiguration making possible an ultimate affirmation and an ultimate joy. This is a joy and an affirmation now ultimately calling us, and calling us from the very center of our abyss; therefore, it is inseparable from that abyss, even if that call is a call to an absolute transfiguration of abyss itself. This is a call to which we are now called theologically, but the immediate task is to open a theological way to that calling, which is the real purpose of this book.

Almost forty years have elapsed since the original writing of *The Gospel of Christian Atheism*, and my theology has evolved considerably since that time. Nevertheless, I think that there is a genuine continuity between my earlier and my later work, and above all so in its centering upon a uniquely Christian atheism. *The New Gospel of Christian Atheism* does incorporate material from my later work, and most particularly so my later understanding of the Christian epic tradition, which I believe is the most decisive way into that ultimate transformation of Christianity that has indeed occurred, and occurred both interiorly and historically, even if that transformation is unknown to all our established or given theologies. Today all forms of Christian orthodoxy can only maintain themselves by refusing any possible ultimate transformation of Christianity, but a radical Christian theology is inevitably in quest of such a transformation, and while commonly this quest occurs in genuine solitude, it also occurs communally. Once again, I am grateful for the critical responses of Robert Detweiler, Lissa McCullough, and Brian Schoeder, and for the truly gracious support of The Davies Group.

T.J.J.A.
2002

Dr. Andrew D. Burbanks has for several years worked as a mathematical artist, producing posters, web sites, and book illustrations. This work includes a series of posters that were displayed on England's London Underground subway system as part of World Mathematical Year 2000.

He is currently involved in research in mathematics, particularly the visualization of systems in more than three dimensions.

Dr. Burbanks can be contacted by email at burbs@aburbs.com and further information can be obtained from his website http://www.aburbs.com/

Introduction

Is a genuine theology possible in our new world? Or a genuinely Christian theology? This book is an exploration of the possibility of a truly new theology for us, one only possible as the consequence of the dissolution of an old theology, a dissolution ending every theology that we have known, or, if not ending it, so profoundly transforming theology itself that only a truly new theology is now possible. But this is a possibility which all of our given or manifest theologies have refused; orthodoxy now reigns in our theological worlds as it has never done since the ending of the medieval world, an orthodoxy which is a profound reaction against the modern world, and above all against a uniquely modern realization of the death of God. The death of God is a truly paradoxical symbol, one which is at once a uniquely Christian and a uniquely modern symbol, a symbol evoking that Crucifixion which the Christian knows as the one source of redemption, and a symbol of that uniquely modern atheism which is a full dissolution or reversal of Christianity. Our deepest thinkers and visionaries of the death of God have effected this ultimate negation through a uniquely Christian language and symbolism, as witness Hegel and Nietzsche, and Blake and Joyce. Such an ultimate atheism is surely possible only within a Christian horizon, or only as a consequence of the ending of Christendom. Paul is the first Christian theologian, if not the first truly individual theologian in the world, and Paul's theology is centered upon the Crucifixion, and upon the Crucifixion as apocalypse itself, an apocalypse which is the very center of an original Christianity, but one which is almost immediately transformed in ancient Christianity, giving us a Christianity which at bottom is either non-apocalyptic or anti-apocalyptic, and that can be understood as the most ultimate transformation of a new religious world that has ever occurred.

Yet a genuine rebirth and renewal of ancient apocalypticism has occurred in the modern world, and paradoxically most fully occurred in our most atheistic movements and enactments, for apocalypticism is truly reborn in Hegel, Marx, and Nietzsche, just as it is in Blake and Joyce, and not simply apocalypticism, but a uniquely Christian apocalypticism. Hegel is our first apocalyptic philosopher, even as Blake is our first fully modern apocalyptic visionary, and yet each enacted an ultimate death of God, and did so in their purest apocalyptic enactments, enactments truly bringing an old world to an end, and even thereby realizing an absolute new world. So, too, Nietzsche's proclamation of the death of God is a truly apocalyptic proclamation, one absolutely ending an old world or an old totality, and calling forth a new heaven and a new earth. If only because of these uniquely modern apocalyptic enactments, we can understand how theology could have become so deeply anti-apocalyptic in the late modern world, and this despite the historical discovery in the late nineteenth century of the apocalyptic Jesus. Blake discovered an apocalyptic Jesus well before this, but Blake's Jesus is a truly revolutionary Jesus, a revolutionary Jesus who has never entered modern Christian dogma, or perhaps any Christian dogma at all.

This book will engage the possibility that Christianity has truly been reborn in the modern world, a rebirth only possible with the ending of Christendom. This is the rebirth of a truly new Christianity, one vastly removed from its ancient and medieval counterparts, and also wholly distant from all given or manifest Christianity, or every Christianity which is commonly known as such. Such an engagement is impossible apart from an ultimate struggle with every manifest theology, or certainly every orthodox theology, a struggle which could only be a theological struggle, and hence one centering upon the uniquely Christian God and the uniquely Christian Christ. But radical theology has seemingly ended with the advent of postmodernity, or if not ended is deeply disguised, and just as postmodernity is giving us a new and comprehensive political conservatism, it is giving us such a theological conservatism as well, and so much so that now the only possible theology is seemingly an orthodox theology. This is a deep transformation of everything that we have known as theology in the modern world, and one threatening to bring all possible modern theology to an end, this is accompanied by an ever more progressive banishment of theology from the academic world, and by a dissolution of all attention to theology in both our major publishers and the mass media. Is theology only possible today as a purely anachronistic enterprise, or only taken seriously by our most reactionary movements, or our most conservative thinkers? This is an extraordinarily different situation of theology than that which was true only a generation ago, and perhaps this truly new theological situation most clearly unveils postmodernity, a postmodernity not only bringing a theological world to an end, but ending everything that we once knew as an ultimate ground.

Of course, theology is very different from our other disciplines, and so much so that perhaps it is not a genuine discipline at all, it is inseparable from what Kierkegaard knew as interiority or "subjectivity," and it intends to draw forth the most ultimate response. There are very good reasons why theology is alien to a new academic world, a genuine theology cannot intend to be "objective," just as it cannot forswear any possible absolute, or be truly independent of all historical traditions. Moreover, theology at bottom intends to engage everyone, and engage everyone in their deepest ground, it cannot possibly be neutral in this engagement, just as it cannot avoid the most absolute claims. For all of these reasons and others theology is now a very lonely enterprise, yet genuine theology claims to speak for everyone, just as it knows its own voyage as one enacted by everyone, and even if this should occur unconsciously or unwittingly, occur it does, and above all so in everything which we can know as either an ultimate judgment or an ultimate liberation. Perhaps the one arena in our academic world which is not closed to theology is literary studies, for our deeper literature inevitably calls forth a theological ground, indeed, much if not most of our more purely theological thinking has occurred among literary scholars, and even if this is unrecognizable as theology to our orthodox theologians, it is certainly not unrecognizable as such to our literary scholars themselves.

Theology is also a self-lacerating enterprise, and above all so a uniquely Christian theology, not only is it an inquiry into the ultimacy of sin, but even thereby it is an inquiry into an eternal death, a death more primal as an actual death than it is in any other tradition, and a death more central in Christian theology than it is in any other theology. Only Christianity knows its lord as a crucified lord, and only Christianity knows a redemption inseparable from the full actualization of an absolute death, and while it is true that there is only a muted thinking about that death in ancient and medieval Christianity, and that the crucifixion only all too gradually enters Christian iconography, with the waning of the medieval world, the crucifixion becomes ever more central in Christianity, and then genuine theological thinking ever more fully thinks the crucifixion. That thinking is inevitably a self-lacerating thinking, one fundamentally occurring in Luther, but no less so in Pascal, and if Kierkegaard is our most self-lacerating thinker, it is Kierkegaard who most purely thinks the crucifixion. While Hegel far more comprehensively thinks the crucifixion than does Kierkegaard, it is Hegel who even thereby first understood an absolute self-alienation, and if that self-alienation is a primal ground of full modernity, it can only be understood through a truly self-lacerating thinking, and it is just such a thinking which is the theological thinking of a full or late modernity.

Inevitably, modern theological thinking is understood as a pathological thinking, a thinking of that pathology which Kierkegaard knew as a sickness unto death, and there can be no innocent thinking of this pathology, none which is not deeply engaged with it, and none which is free of the profound scars which are thereby incurred. Such scars can be a genuine sign of theology, and while they can be truly repulsive to the non-theologian, they are a genuine mark of a Christian theological voyage, or of a deeper Christian theological voyage, and this is true not only of the modern theological world, but of the ancient Christian world as well. Augustine created a theological revolution by discovering self-consciousness itself, but that is a wholly guilty self-consciousness, one inseparable from the "bad conscience" itself, and while it is the one arena for us of grace, a uniquely Christian grace occurs only through an ultimate judgment, and a judgment absolutely assaulting the very center of consciousness. Hence to be open to that center, or to inquire into that center, is to be open to that assault, an assault making manifest those interior chains which most enslave us, chains it is true which made possible Augustine's discovery of an interior freedom, but that is a freedom only knowable by knowing an interior bondage. One cannot know that bondage apart from an interior realization of bondage itself, and if that is the way to a Christian understanding of grace, or a Western Christian understanding of grace, it is inseparable from a genuine if not an ultimate self-laceration.

But today theology is most offensive or most alien because it is a thinking of God, and while many if not most theologians now disguise this, theology cannot be theology apart from a thinking of God, and yet that is the very thinking which is most alien in our world. However, we inherit a tradition in which thinking is necessarily and essentially a thinking of God. Not until Hume and Kant is there a major philosophical thinker who is not a fully theological thinker, and Kant could only be an ethical thinker by being a theological thinker, so it is that Heidegger can understand the Western philosophical tradition as ontotheology, a tradition which does not end until Nietzsche. Then it appears to end decisively, being almost wholly absent from twentieth century philosophy, although theology itself does recur in Heidegger's major work, *Being and Time*, which can understand human existence or *Dasein* only through fallenness, *Angst*, and death, yet here theology recurs wholly apart from a thinking of "God." Heidegger did make possible Levinas and Derrida, and here a return of theology to philosophy occurs, although this is a deeply muted or elusive thinking of the "Infinite," and one which never openly or fully thinks God. That may well be because of the deeply Jewish and aniconic ground of Levinas and Derrida, one absent in Whitehead, the only other major twentieth century philosopher who thinks God, but this occurs only in the late Whitehead, a Whitehead who only affected theology and not philosophy itself. Only twentieth century philosophy is not a thinking of God, for Nietzsche thinks God if only in thinking the death of God, and nothing is so distinctive or unique in twentieth century philosophical thinking as is the absence of God.

Karl Barth, the most influential theologian of the twentieth century, brought philosophical theology to an end, and now it is open and alive only in the Catholic world, but that is a world now caught up in a profoundly reactionary movement, and its most powerful theologians are under assault. And the truth is that all theologians are now under assault, theology can be understood as our most precarious vocation, the one most in danger of extinction, if that has not already occurred. Why should this be so? Apparently religion is more powerful in the world today than it was a century ago, it certainly comprehends far more people, now even politicians assume a religious voice in addressing the public, blasphemy has virtually disappeared from our public discourse, and "atheists" are seemingly very rare if not non-existent. This, too, is a paradoxical situation, for just as fundamentalism throughout the world can know our dominant world as an atheistic world, the very word 'God' is more absent from our language than it has ever previously been, virtually never being spoken in our serious discourse, and then commonly only with apology or embarrassment. Even the most religious among us have little interest in theology, fundamental theology is disappearing from our theological schools, and our theological publishers are ever more fully restricting the publication of theology. Is theology now a forbidden discourse, and one now only present in artifacts of a distant and irrecoverable past?

Yet is it actually possible to end theology? Is it truly possible to avoid all thinking of God, and not simply to numb or disguise it, but to end it altogether? The very fury with which Communism opposed theology in a seemingly atheistic world is one sign to the contrary, just as the deep hostility towards theology of our dominant philosophical world is another, so, too, it is extraordinarily difficult even in a postmodern world to discover a literature with no theological ground at all, or any form of art which is truly and finally atheological. Perhaps the very idea of the atheological is our purest illusion, and while it could be employed by Derrida, Derrida's most recent work is truly and openly theological, and if Heidegger truly is the major philosopher of the twentieth century, Heidegger never abandoned theological thinking, or even attempted to do so. Wittgenstein himself can be understood as a theologian by some of his most astute interpreters, and now we know that his life itself was inseparable from a theological quest, is every such quest now ended, or is it far rather more deeply disguised? Is this a mask which we must now wear, and one disguising our theological quest even from ourselves, for is this a quest which now must be so solitary as to bear no mark whatsoever of itself? Our most deeply anti-theological thinkers, and above all Nietzsche himself, could never escape or even transcend a theological language, and Nietzsche could know that it is the very grammar of our language which necessarily binds us to God.

Perhaps it is "God" whom we have most deeply repressed, that one whom it is most forbidden for us to name, and if this is a uniquely modern or postmodern condition, we cannot transcend this condition apart from a naming of God, a naming of God which is inevitably a theological naming. What most blocks us here is the conviction that theology can only be a conservative or orthodox theology, or that there can be no theology which is not an ecclesiastical theology, no theology which is not generated by a religious institution or body. While this is clearly not true in the pre-Christian world, and above all untrue in ancient Greece, it is also untrue with the full advent of modernity, already Milton was an anti-ecclesiastical theologian, and this becomes far deeper in Schelling, Hegel, and Kierkegaard, so that it is a uniquely modern theological thinking which orthodox theology can know as the deepest enemy of faith. A genuinely modern theological thinking is inevitably a heterodox thinking, so that even Newman can be known as a heretic in conservative Catholic circles, and such circles have gone so far as to identify Rahner as a Satanic thinker, and Satanic because he is a modern theological thinker. Our secular world has virtually no awareness that a radical theology even exists, and while it is now publicly invisible, it remains very much alive insofar as a genuinely modern thinking exists, and while a new postmodernity threatens to end modern thinking, it certainly cannot end modern scientific thinking, and therefore inevitably cannot end modern thinking itself.

This book is written with the conviction that no greater task now lies at hand than a truly new engagement with theology, a new engagement which could only be a radical engagement, and radical if only because of our new condition. While this book has enormous shortcomings, and is all too abbreviated fully to succeed in its purpose, it hopes to advance the cause of a new theology, and to open theology itself to those who are now most deeply alienated from it. Moreover, it is addressed not to the professional theologian, but rather to anyone who is open to theology, or anyone seeking a contemporary theological language and thinking. Few will choose the path that here is followed, but the greater challenge is simply to open a theological path for us, no doubt many such paths are now possible, but they are hidden from view, or not yet explored. Simply following one such path will hopefully open other vistas, and while they may well be at hand, they are now virtually invisible, or visible only to a very few. While the path here followed is an explicitly Christian one, it seeks a new Christianity which is a universal Christianity, and not the Christianity of a universal Church, but far rather one of a universal body, a universal body which is an apocalyptic body, and thus the body of Here Comes Everybody.

Chapter One

The Uniqueness of Christianity

Religion

The advent of the new world of the third millennium has unveiled in yet another perspective a Christianity that is anything but new; perhaps never before has Christianity been so bereft of any possible sign of the new, if only thereby it is a reversal of an original Christianity, a Christianity that could know and proclaim itself as the absolutely new. The very symbol of *absolute novum* was born in Christianity, a symbol originally enacted in Jesus' proclamation of the advent of the Kingdom of God, and just as this is the very center of the acts and words of Jesus, it is a center inseparable from what Christianity knows as the new creation, that new æon that is apocalypse itself. Hence original Christianity was a revolutionary movement towards an absolutely new future, as for the first time a movement was born that was wholly and totally directed towards an absolutely new future, and only after this birth does there arise an actual movement towards a truly new future in history itself. Is there any sign of that revolutionary movement in contemporary Christianity, any witness here to a truly new world, even any opening to a genuinely new millennium, or any awareness of the truly new at all? If not, is this a decisive sign of a profound transformation of Christianity, and even if this occurred over two millennia, is it nevertheless a genuine sign of a Christianity that has truly reversed itself?

Christianity can know itself as being truly and even absolutely unique, as first proclaimed by Paul, hence the necessity not only of Christianity's break from what it can know as an "old" covenant and an "old" Torah, but also the necessity of its ultimate challenge to the world itself, which was inevitably a challenge to the Roman Empire. While in genuine continuity with an original prophetic assault upon "paganism," this challenge can now call forth the fullness of the world itself as "pagan," a world that it can know as an "old world," an old world absolutely opposed to the new, hence a truly demonic world, and one whose lord is Satan. Christ is the lord of the new creation or the new æon, an absolutely new world that has now dawned, a dawning that soon will bring an end to the old æon or the old creation. This induces in the Christian an ecstatic joy, a joy in the advent of the absolutely new, and a joy inseparable from that very advent. Has all such joy now vanished from the Christian world, and vanished in a Christian world that is closed to the new, and above all closed to the very possibility of the absolutely new?

If only in this perspective, it is imperative that we become open to the genuine uniqueness of Christianity, a uniqueness perhaps invisible today as it has never been before. Has Christianity finally reached the point at which it is in no sense whatsoever a genuine ground of a truly new future? Is that a fundamental reason for the contemporary invisibility of its uniqueness? Has Christianity truly inverted itself by becoming grounded only in an ancient world, or only in truly previous or "old" worlds, and does that impel Christianity towards a fundamental and ultimate movement of return, an ultimate return that could only be an eternal return? Eternal return itself is the domain of the most ancient or the most primordial religion, an archaic religion that for many millennia was quite simply religion itself, and a primordial return is not only a cyclical return, but is an ultimately backward moving return to a primordial totality, and here the only possible ultimate movement is one of *return*. This is the eternal return that was shattered by the prophetic revolution of Israel. The prophetic assault upon paganism was an assault upon the archaic movement of eternal return, one that for the first time opened the horizon of an ultimate future, an ultimate future that is possible only by way of an ultimate negation of the past, or an ultimate negation of what now for the first time can be known as an "old," which is truly other than the "new." The reform prophets could know a monarchic covenant and a monarchic cultus as being truly "old," or truly pagan, hence they assaulted both a monarchic covenant and a priestly cultus as ultimate rebellions against Yahweh, rebellions now culminating in an absolute judgment, and an absolute judgment ending an "old" Israel. Only this judgment makes possible a truly "new" Israel, and for the first time a call to an absolutely new world is enacted, hence the prophetic revolution is truly apocalyptic, marking the advent of a full and genuine apocalypticism. This became the apocalypticism that was the womb of Christianity, and there is no more radical expression of the prophetic revolution than Jesus himself, a truly apocalyptic Jesus, and one giving birth to the truly and ultimately apocalyptic Paul.

Apocalypticism is the very inversion of the movement of eternal return, for it is a forward movement to an absolute future rather than a backward movement to an absolute or primordial past. Its goal is an absolutely new omega rather than an absolutely primordial past, and the fullness of an apocalyptic movement can be known by the degree to which it knows and enacts that absolute future as being already dawning or present. Thus a genuinely apocalyptic movement is the very opposite of an archaic or primordial movement of eternal return, and an original apocalyptic Christianity embodies a total assault upon every movement of eternal return. But, has that assault been reversed in a post-apocalyptic Christianity, and reversed even by way of a comprehensive renewal of the movement of eternal return? Historians of religion can know eternal return as a universal religious movement, one clearly manifest even in Judaism, Christianity, and Islam, but apocalypticism has been deeply heterodox in all of these monotheistic traditions, and most so in Christianity, despite Christianity's apocalyptic origin. Is Christianity alone among the world religions at war with its own origin, is it Christianity alone that has profoundly transformed its very origin, and is that a genuine uniqueness of Christianity?

Twentieth century dialectical theology can know Christianity as the absolute opposite of religion itself, hence Barth's total assault upon religion in his revolutionary commentary on Romans, but does such a theological understanding have a genuine historical ground? Is the ultimate uniqueness of Christianity one that is historically or actually manifest? An investigation of this question can most clearly occur by contrasting Christianity with those religious worlds that are most distant from it; surely these comprehend the great religions of the Orient, and above all that Oriental mysticism that is truly universal in these traditions. We must recognize immediately that this is a mysticism truly alien to us, and alien not only because of its universality in its own world, but also because of its very purity, a purity not to be found in the Christian world where a deeper mysticism has always been under assault, inevitably driven into an opposing underground, and never allowed a fully open expression. Moreover, Oriental mysticism can embody a totality that is truly alien to Christian mysticism, a totality embodying every dimension of life whatsoever, and one expressing itself in a comprehensive philosophy wherein a deeply mystical intuition can realize itself as pure thinking itself, a thinking never known in Western Christianity, so at this point a genuine chasm appears between East and West. Nowhere in the Orient can we apprehend what the West has known as either God or Being, or nowhere in truly Oriental traditions, a "Being" or "God" simply impossible either in purely mystical ways or in truly total ways, ways dissolving every ultimate difference whatsoever.

The very symbol of totality is illuminating here, for even if it has appeared again and again in the West, it has always done so as an heretical or heterodox power, and never does it appear in the West with the purity of Oriental traditions. Western visions of totality have always been profoundly heterodox, a heterodoxy unknown in the East, and just as Christian epic enactments of totality have been deeply if not purely heretical, and ever more heretical as they evolve, a genuine Western thinking of totality has been no less heterodox, as in Spinoza, Hegel, and Nietzsche. Yet nowhere in the West have we been given either a genuine vision or a genuine understanding of a truly primordial totality, a totality that is not only all in all, but an undifferentiated totality, and one manifest only in an absolute calm or an absolute quiescence. Such a quiescence and calm are truly alien to the West, as is an absolute silence, a silence that is simply unspeakable in a Western language, and truly alien to everything that the West has known as either word or speech. The historian of religions can know paradise as a universal symbol, but there are profound differences between what the East and the West have known as paradise. The West has never been able to envision a truly primordial paradise, one fully called forth in Eastern vision, and a pure or original innocence is truly alien to the West, a West that can only actually know innocence as an innocence lost. Inevitably, Eastern vision is exotic to the West, and not only exotic but truly unreal, but that very "unreality" illuminates the uniqueness of Christianity, a Christianity inseparable from an ultimately fallen or opposing actuality.

The Orient can know an ultimate identity of *nirvana* and *samsara*, or of "Being" and "nothingness," or of life and death, so that both Far Eastern and Indian Buddhists employ words whose immediate reference is to non-being and nothingness when they speak of *Nirvana* or *Sunyata*, and if only for this reason there is no possibility of an apprehension here of what the West has known as either Being or God. Finally Heidegger himself came to recognize that everything that is known as Being in the West is absent in the East, but this is already demonstrated in Hegel's lectures on the philosophy of religion, and perhaps nothing else has so deeply challenged Christianity's claim to universality, or so ultimately challenged every possible scholastic theology. While apocalypticism is seemingly present in the East, it is very different from Western apocalypticism; nowhere in the East does an absolute assault upon an "old" world or an "old" totality occur, and there is no recognition in the East of an eternal return as an eternal *return*, for even if the practice of Yoga is a praxis reversing consciousness itself, making possible an interior recovery of an absolutely original condition, that 'original' condition is not original in any Western sense, for it is identical with the fullness of the present itself. What the West has known as the very actuality of time is truly absent in the East, here there is no ultimate or fully actual difference between present, past, and future, hence no possibility of what the

West has known as eternal return, or what the West has known as an absolute or apocalyptic future.

So, too, the primordial itself has a very different meaning in the East than it does in the West, and, indeed, is not primordial in any Western sense, for it is just as fully actual in the present as in the past, and in that sense is not past at all. In the East, there is no possibility of an ultimate difference of any kind, neither temporally nor spatially, so there can be no "here" that is truly different from a "there," and consequently no possibility of anything that the West has known as "will." We can know Eastern ways as dissolving all actual or willful movement, whether by way of the *wu wei* of Taoism and Zen, or the Yogic discipline of emptying the contents of consciousness, or the purposeless action of the *Bhagavad-Gita*. In an Eastern perspective these ways are not inactivations of the will, a will that itself is wholly illusory, but rather recoveries or renewals of our actual condition, or of life itself. Neither are they recoveries or renewals in any Western sense, for nothing has actually been lost; all seeming loss is only an illusion, and even if pain and suffering are real, and universally real, they are finally real only as an illusion, an illusion that an Oriental redemption wholly dissolves. Yet nothing actually happens or occurs in that redemption, for it is nothing more than a disillusion, a loss of all possible illusion, and that illusion is wholly and absolutely unreal. Clearly, the very identity of the "real" is truly different in East and West, and each is wholly "unreal" from the perspective of the other.

Just as nostalgia is truly absent from the East, a nostalgia that has consumed the West, there can be no longing in the East for a lost paradise, for paradise is here and now and nowhere else. Only in illusion can we imagine a lost paradise, an illusion that is dissolved when paradise is actually discovered, but that is not a discovery in any Western sense, it is at bottom a realization of what we have always most deeply and most purely known. Yes, we can forget what we most purely know, and that forgetting is a universal condition, but it is only a forgetting, and not an actual loss or perishing. Hence there is no possibility here of anything that Christianity has known as fall, nor any possibility of what Christianity knows as the Creator or the creation, or any possibility of what Christianity knows as redemption. All of these are purely and finally an illusion from an Oriental perspective, and above all so from a Buddhist perspective, and even if Buddhism is that Oriental way that is seemingly closest to Christianity, it is ultimately more distant from Christianity than any other way, for it is Buddhism more purely than any other way that makes the Christian God absolutely impossible. Of course, there are true parallels between Buddhism and Christianity; each know their redeemers as a total embodiment of compassion, just as each can know their redeemers as the one source of redemption, but a Buddhist redemption is a realization of "reality" itself, whereas a Christian redemption is a realization of an absolutely new or an absolutely "other" reality, a reality that is the absolute opposite of everything that is real in a truly or wholly fallen world.

Therefore, Christianity knows an absolute dichotomy or an absolute opposition that is simply impossible in Buddhism, an opposition between the depths of sin and the depths of grace, depths of grace inseparable from the depths of sin, for they are depths of grace only realizable in the depths of sin, and only an absolute opposition or an absolute dichotomy between sin and grace makes possible a uniquely Christian redemption. Buddhism is liberated from any possible awareness of fall, or any awareness of a real or actual fall, but Christianity is inseparable from an absolute fall, a fall wholly transforming the creation, now an infinite gulf or chasm is realized between God and the world, as a truly new world dawns, and dawns as a truly fallen world, and it is in that fallen world that a Christian redemption occurs. Only this fallenness makes possible the "realism" of the Western Christian world, a realism knowing a truly autonomous world. Only then can space and time be truly actual as an autonomous time and space, and only then can humanity stand forth as an autonomous humanity, a humanity wholly unknown in Buddhism, and unknown in the world itself until the advent of Christianity. Yet that advent itself is the realization of an absolute fall, only now can the world itself be known as a wholly fallen world, and only now can a grace be known that is absolutely inseparable from an absolutely fallen world.

No perspective is more distant from this perspective than a Buddhist one, and if Buddhism is the purest dissolution of dualism that the world has ever known, it is absolutely closed to every possibility of otherness itself, hence absolutely closed to the Christian God, and not only to the Christian God but to the Christian world, as fully manifest in the vast distance between Buddhist and Western philosophy. Only in Spinoza has Western philosophy wholly overcome dualism, but Spinoza is the most isolated and marginalized philosopher in the West, whereas a Buddhist philosophical dissolution of dualism can be known as the very center of Oriental philosophy, and just as this fully occurs in Mahayana Buddhism, it is Mahayana Buddhism that is the most universal way in the Orient. True, it is Mahayana Buddhism that is the fullest realization of an absolute nothingness in the East, one with no real parallel anywhere in the West, but a Buddhist absolute nothingness is an absolute totality, and as such can be understood as an ultimate dissolution of every possible dualism. So there is no possible Nihil in Buddhism, no Nothing that is the opposite of the real, but far rather a "Nothing" that is reality itself, and a reality that Mahayana Buddhism knows as *Sunyata*. What could be further from this reality than a uniquely Western realism, or a uniquely Christian God, or a uniquely Christian grace? Is it possible that Buddhism is the very opposite of Christianity, and an opposite truly unveiling Christianity itself, an unveiling which is the unveiling of the uniqueness of Christianity?

Perhaps it is a uniquely Christian Gnosticism that most clearly makes manifest the ultimate distance between Buddhism and Christianity, for even if Gnosticism is an ultimate Christian heterodoxy, it can now be known as originating in Christianity, and certainly Gnosticism has again and again returned in Christianity, and returned even in a Christian orthodoxy that knows eternal life and eternal life alone. Far more fully than elsewhere in the West, the Gnostic way is a way of eternal return, and even a return to an unfallen Godhead, for it is Gnosticism that first knows the fall of Godhead itself, a fall activating or making possible the Creator, a Creator whom the Gnostic can name as Ialdabaoth or Satan, and a Creator who is the absolute opposite of a uniquely Gnostic redeemer. In Gnosticism, an eternal return occurs only by way of a violent assault upon the world, one with no parallel in the East, no truly pure or immediate way of return is possible in Gnosticism, just as there cannot be a genuinely Gnostic art or a genuinely Gnostic philosophy, or not in anything that the Christian world has known as Gnosticism. Moreover, Gnostic language is derived and second-hand, as fully manifest in Gnostic mythology; and ingenious as that mythology may well be, no one cold imagine it as an historical mythology, or one that has ever been a living mythology. Surely Gnosticism is a genuine witness to the consequences of a total Christian movement into eternal return, and while Gnosticism is extraordinarily powerful in Christianity, it would be impossible in Buddhism, and impossible if only because Gnosticism is our ultimate dualism, a dualism absolutely impossible in Buddhism.

Now it is true that a dissolution or reversal of dualism has been an ultimate goal of the West, or certainly of the Christian West, but is this a goal that has ever been achieved, or achieved in anything but our most ultimate heterodoxy? And could this be achieved apart from an absolute transformation of everything that the Christian world has known as Godhead itself, and if a Buddhist *Sunyata* is most distant from everything that is given or manifest to the West as the Godhead, could that *Sunyata* be a model or a paradigm of an absolutely transfigured Christian Godhead, a Godhead in which Being *is* an absolute nothingness, but an absolute nothingness that is an absolutely transfiguring nothingness? This is a Godhead already apprehended by a deeper Christian mysticism, but one never called forth in the fuller expressions of Western Christianity, unless this occurs in heterodoxies so radical that they have yet to be theologically understood. Perhaps the East can offer an horizon making possible such an ultimate theological transformation. Surely it is in the perspective of the East that we can most clearly see the uniqueness of Christianity, but is that a perspective in which we can see the way to a genuine theological revolution, and a revolution absolutely transforming everything that we can now understand as the uniquely Christian Godhead?

History

Eternal return in all of its multiple expressions is inevitably a cyclical movement, and a cyclical movement necessarily annulling or dissolving all actual particularity or uniqueness. Here history itself can only be manifest as a movement of eternal return, as manifest in all archaic records and documents. Such eternal return is not truly or actually challenged until the advent of Israel, and not ultimately challenged until the occurrence of the prophetic revolution, a revolution first realizing an ultimate break or chasm between the future and the past. Now the future, or the ultimate future, is truly and wholly other than the past, and a call to that future can only occur by decisively breaking or dissolving any call of eternal return, a breakage or dissolution inevitably calling forth an absolutely new actuality of time itself. This is an actuality of time impossible in the movement of eternal return, hence it is not found in those worlds grounded in an eternal return, worlds comprehending the world itself until the advent of Israel, although only in the course of many centuries did Israel dissolve or transform the movement of eternal return. Messianism is illuminating here, for while it is found throughout the world, not until Israel is it divorced from the movement of eternal return, and even if Israel primarily knows the messiah by way of an archaic imagery of sacred kingship, the Israelitic messiah is a truly new monarch reversing any possible archaic world, and doing so if only because this messiah is a truly and even absolutely future messiah.

This reversal of archaic monarchy is most unique and most powerful in the radically new image of the messiah or the redeemer as the suffering servant, an absolutely new redeemer deeply resisted by Israel, just as it was by the disciples of Jesus, but most resisted and opposed by virtually the whole body of orthodox or traditional Christianity. Jesus opposed the whole horizon of the messianic expectations that he met, and opposed it most by his proclamation and enactment of a dawning Kingdom of God. This is the very kingdom that is almost immediately transformed by Christianity, and wholly transformed by understanding the kingdom of God as the absolute sovereignty and the absolute transcendence of God, a transcendent sovereignty truly other than that dawning kingdom that Jesus enacted and proclaimed. Thereby, the forward movement of an apocalyptic kingdom is reversed into the backward movement of eternal return. The sacrificial or self-emptying way of the suffering servant is reversed by knowing a Christ who is absolute power and absolute glory, and the incarnate movement of a dawning Kingdom of God is reversed into an ascending movement directed to an absolutely primordial Godhead. Moreover, if this is a genuine renewal or resurrection of eternal return, it is so only by way of an ultimate reversal, and an ultimate reversal of a purely apocalyptic movement towards an absolute and revolutionary future.

Historical Christianity is a truly dichotomous Christianity, one torn asunder by conflicting and opposing forces as no other historical movement or tradition has been. Here one can encounter both absolute power and absolute sacrifice, both an absolutely apocalyptic future and an absolutely primordial past, both an ultimate and unchallengeable law and authority and a pure antinomianism, both revolutionary transformation and a profoundly conservative or reactionary power. No other tradition has been so deeply at war with itself, or generated such ultimate and comprehensive heterodoxies, or known an orthodoxy so pure or so authoritative, an orthodoxy generating pure heterodoxies, even as an original Christian apocalypticism generated Christian orthodoxy. Until the advent of modern totalitarianism, an absolute intolerance was known only in Christianity, but this intolerance is more profoundly an internal rather than an external one, one most directed at the deepest of all enemies, who can only be enemies within. Paul could discover a new self-consciousness by knowing a profoundly internal dichotomy, an apocalyptic war between *sarx* and *pneuma* or "flesh" and Spirit, and a war that would soon be universalized in a new Christian world. This is a world initiating the most dynamic of all historical worlds, as most clearly manifest in Christianity's own profound transformations, transformations inseparable from a deep internal discord, and an internal discord ever enlarging itself; no other world finally embodies such ultimate internal oppositions. These very oppositions finally generated a uniquely Christian secularization, a pure and total secularization occurring only in a Christian or post-Christian world or worlds, and a secularization once again releasing ultimate oppositions, oppositions that can be understood as a uniquely Christian sign or signature. Only in a Christian or in a post-Christian world is an ultimate dichotomy manifest and real, one both external and internal, a dichotomy embodying an absolute opposition, an opposition between real and actual opposites, and one that can be stilled only by an ultimate impotence or passivity.

Dichotomy itself is a decisive key unveiling the uniqueness of Christianity, one clearly manifest in Christology itself, a Christology affirming the full and integral union of the humanity and the divinity of Christ, but never has such a union been truly or actually known in anything given to us as Christian theology, and this because all established Christian understanding has never been able to escape or to transcend a chasm or a gulf between humanity and divinity, an uncrossable gulf between a full and actual humanity and Godhead itself. Thus Christianity embodies a truly paradoxical relationship between humanity and divinity. Just as no other tradition has known such a profound union between humanity and the Godhead, so none has known such an overwhelming chasm between Godhead and the world. Just as Christianity has been profoundly world-affirming and profoundly world-negating at once, it has known a Christ or a Redeemer who is fully flesh and fully Spirit simultaneously, and if only thereby a truly dichotomous Christ. So, too, has Christianity known consciousness itself as a truly dichotomous consciousness, a self-consciousness that is truly free and truly impotent or enslaved at once, and if an internal freedom does not dawn in the world until the advent of Christianity, this freedom is known only by knowing the impotence or enslavement of the will, an internal and interior bondage or self-bondage making manifest the freedom of the will. Yet, that freedom is enclosed within a wholly fallen will that can only be redeemed by an eternal predestination. That predestination is simultaneously a predestination of absolute judgment and absolute redemption, and a redemption that can only be known through knowing an absolute judgment. Hence a uniquely Christian freedom is inseparable from a uniquely Christian guilt, one in which consciousness itself is inevitably a guilty conscience, as an absolute guilt is born that is inseparable from the historical epiphany of the uniquely Christian God.

If a Christian incarnation is truly unique, and unique as an incarnation in the "flesh," that "flesh" is inseparable from the actuality of history, or the actuality of the world itself, so that the incarnate Christ is the fully actual Christ, but only as the consequence of a divine and ultimate movement of incarnation. This is an actuality of Christ that is annulled and reversed by Christian movements of ascension and return, and that very reversal unveils the absolute newness of that actuality that is realized by the Incarnation, an *absolute novum* so absolutely challenging as to impel its own reversal, thereby releasing a truly new and ultimate movement of eternal return. Now eternal return can only be a return to primordial Godhead, and an absolutely primordial Godhead, one never previously manifest in the West, and one only called forth by the full advent of Christianity. Only now does the very symbol and idea of the Godhead dawn in the consciousness of the West, just as only now is an absolute infinitude manifest for the first time, one truly alien to Greek philosophy, and an absolutely new infinitude releasing a new and comprehensive other-worldliness, a truly new other-worldliness that can be understood as being only possible by way of a reversal of a uniquely Christian incarnation. Hence, *absolute novum* can call forth its true opposite, an opposite that is an absolutely primordial Godhead, thereby a genuine dichotomy between *absolute novum* and the absolutely primordial becomes actual and real, and historically real in the full actualization of Christianity.

We know that no other tradition begins with such a deep internal division and conflict, and it is now possible to see that Gnosticism has its origin in primitive Christianity, for there is no historical evidence of a pre-Christian Gnosticism, but there is historical evidence in the Pauline and Johannine epistles of a deep conflict with Gnosticism then occurring in Christianity, and this was perhaps the deepest of all conflicts in primitive Christianity. A conflict between Gnosticism and apocalypticism is an ultimate conflict between an absolute future and the absolutely primordial, a conflict soon generating a uniquely Christian orthodoxy, and an orthodoxy that was a negation of apocalypt-icism and Gnosticism at once. Thus Christianity begins with an ultimate trans-formation, a beginning found nowhere else in the world, but, so, too, Christianity fully transforms itself as it evolves, and while a comparable transformation occurs in Islam, never in Islam are there such compre-hensive conflicts about the Godhead as in Christianity, and nothing truly comparable in Islam to the ultimate Christological conflicts in Christianity. Certainly Islam does not know a dichotomy in Godhead itself, but Christianity has always known a dichotomous Christ, a Christ who is the primordial Logos and the apocalyptic Redeemer, a Christ who is absolute power and majesty, and the wholly sacrificial Christ who is the kenotic or self-emptying Christ, a Christ who is the universal Christ and a Christ who is known in the Church alone. Never are these conflicts truly resolved in Christianity, for they occur again and again, and are most absent in the least powerful expressions of Christianity, and if all such conflict has now ended in Christianity, that would be yet another sign of a Christianity that has truly reversed itself.

A truly new Christianity has been born in late modernity, one for the first time giving us a theology of the Church and of the Church alone, and only now does Christianity become truly isolated from the world, or from every forward movement in the world, a Christianity closed to *novum* itself, and above all closed to that *absolute novum* that was born with the advent of Christianity. Today it is only historians, and commonly secular historians, who can call forth the power and the riches of Christendom, a power truly vanishing from the contemporary

Church, except as it is present in relics and artifacts. Genuine theology can now maintain only a very precarious existence in the Church, and there has seemingly vanished every contemporary Christian art and every contemporary Christian philosophy. For the first time a fully manifest Christianity can exist only in a truly sectarian form, one wholly directed towards the past, and a Christian past that is now undergoing an ultimate transformation. Only now is a Christian historical past ceasing to be a living past, or a history that can be lived even now in a creative moment, and a history in genuine continuity with its own future. That is a history inseparable from ultimate and comprehensive transformations, but no such transformation of Christianity is apparently possible today, and this despite the fact that a new world has truly arrived. Is Christianity now possible only as a backward moving way, must it resolutely set itself against every possible revolutionary or forward-moving power, and, if so, could there be a greater reversal of an original Christianity?

Many ironies beset this reversal, such as the common claim of twentieth century theologians that Christianity is a uniquely historical faith, a claim occurring at the very time when all manifest Christianity is more distant from the actualities of history than Christianity had ever previously been. Indeed, since the French Revolution Christianity has progressively moved towards the peripheries of history, or certainly done so in its ecclesiastical expressions. For the first time an ecclesiastical Christianity is fully real that is truly distant from its own world, or distant from the truly creative and powerful expressions of its world, a condition that was not true of a pre-Constantinian Christianity, which was already truly entering and transforming the world. Not until full- or late-modernity does a sectarian Christianity abound, one even profoundly affecting Catholicism itself, a truly new Catholicism finally forced to abandon its absolute opposition to the modern world, and only then facing the crisis of the end of Christendom, an ending making impossible everything that Catholicism has historically become through the Constantinian establishment, and also an ending that is a consequence of a uniquely modern secularization. Can Christianity truly survive the end of Christendom, or survive it as anything but a purely sectarian Christianity, one finally renouncing every Christian promise of transforming the world?

Can we understand that there is a genuine parallel or even a *coincidentia oppositorum* between the beginning and the ending of Christendom? If it is possible to understand that there were Christian forces that generated modern secularization, which theologically could be understood as a consequence of the Incarnation, and that these forces ever more fully evolve in Christian history, is this a necessary consequence of a uniquely Christian realization of an *absolute novum*? And if it is true that it is only after the advent of Christianity that a comprehensive forward movement of history ever more gradually arises, and one inevitably ending the ancient world, does that very movement necessarily entail an ever more progressive transformation of the Christian world, a transformation that is finally a reversal of Christendom? Just as Christianity reversed its original apocalyptic ground in becoming "orthodox" Christianity, can an ultimate movement of reversal be understood as occurring throughout Christian history, and one culminating in the end of Christen-dom? If so, that ending is not the ending of Christianity, but rather a fulfillment of a uniquely Christian history, and one in genuine continuity with its deeper ground, and its deeper historical ground, an historical ground that is a truly revolutionary power. And a revolutionary power as a kenotic or self-emptying power, one that is finally the kenotic or sacrificial body of Christ, and a sacrificial body inseparable from that apocalyptic Spirit that is both the call to and an embodiment of an absolute future or an absolute apocalypse.

New Christianities have arisen again and again in Christian history, and above all so during the great turning points or crises of Christian history, certainly full modernity has brought such a crisis to Christianity, but has that crisis generated a truly new Christianity, and one vastly distant from its predecessors? We can observe such a Christianity in a truly new sectarian Christianity, but is there a deep contrary or even opposite of that Christianity that has been born in full modernity, one at an infinite distance from all sectarian Christianity, and one deeply embodied in a truly new world? Such a Christianity would be invisible as such to all established or given Christianity, and insofar as it is manifest it could only incur an assault from that Christian world. Such assaults have always occurred in response to truly new expressions of Christianity, and if the modern crisis of Christianity is the greatest crisis in Christian history, a new Christianity that is the consequence of that crisis would be far more distant from its predecessors than any new Christianity has previously been. Certainly it would be truly and perhaps even absolutely "new," and in its perspective all given Christianity would not only be "old," but ultimately "old"; not only would a genuine gulf then exist between a new and an old Christianity, but each would be the very opposite of the other. In the sixteenth century, Protestantism and Catholicism could so understand each other, but a far greater gulf now lies between an old and a new Christianity than existed between Catholicism and Protestantism, and perhaps an even greater gulf than that between Catholicism and Gnosticism. If Christian history has inevitably generated ultimate heterodoxies, no greater heterodoxy has ever existed than those generated by the modern world. Newman could discover the development or evolution of Christian doctrine as occurring through an ultimate struggle with heresy, and one leaving heresies behind as dead fossils, so that the very mark of heresy is immobility, as opposed to the forward and living movement of a genuine Christian dogma. Yet we are finally confronted with a Christian dogma that has ceased to move or to evolve, and confronted with ultimate heterodoxies with truly overwhelming power. Is this a sign that an authentically Christian forward or evolving movement is occurring through these heterodoxies, and that the immobility of Christian orthodoxy today is a sign of its ultimately heretical ground?

Only in the modern world is there a realization of the integral and essential relationship between heresy and orthodoxy in Christianity, only then could it be understood how each is inseparable from the other, and how each evolves only by way of a conflict with the other. Yet modern theology refuses to confront our modern heterodoxies as Christian heterodoxies, perhaps because they are so powerful, or so comprehensive, or so irresistible. Certainly modern theology has been driven into an ultimate retreat, but could this be a reaction to a truly new Christianity, a Christianity so new that thus far it has been theologically unnamable? Nevertheless, ultimate Christian heterodoxies such as those of Blake and Hegel are enacted as embodiments of a truly new and even apocalyptic Christianity, and they have had an enormous effect upon the modern world, one that is the very opposite of the impact of an "old" Christianity. At every crucial point such heterodoxies truly reverse Christian orthodoxy, and thereafter Christian orthodoxy truly retreats, or engages in a retrogressive movement, so that today Christian orthodoxy can be known as an ultimately reactionary movement.

Is it possible that the manifest or open Christianity of late modernity and postmodernity is a polar or opposing expression of a truly new and genuinely revolutionary Christianity, a revolutionary Christianity in genuine continuity with Christianity's deeper ground, and one truly embodying that *absolute novum* with which Christianity begins? The open or given Christianity of our world is surely the very opposite of that *novum*, and is that itself a crucial sign of the advent of a truly new Christianity, and is a profound conflict now occurring between an old Christianity and a new Christianity that is a rebirth of that ultimate conflict that occurred with the birth of Christianity? If only the advent of Christianity called forth an ultimate movement of eternal return, and an eternal return most purely embodied in Christian orthodoxy itself, has that return been reborn in our world, and now reborn as a comprehensive historical movement? Is it only in our world that a backward movement of return is most fully manifest and real, and is that an inevitable response to a new and ultimately revolutionary movement, one that is the very opposite of all given Christianity, even as an original Christianity was the very opposite of that world that it encountered? There is no more challenging category than *absolute novum*, but is it realized only with the realization of its very opposite, can it be actual and real only with the advent of its true opposite, an absolutely "old" that is the true opposite of the absolutely "new," and whose realization as a truly and finally old world is only possible with the full actualization of an *absolute novum*?

Death

Only Christianity among the world religions enacts the fullness and the finality of a truly actual death, a death that is an ultimate death, and a death inseparable from what Christianity knows as an absolute fall. Paul could know an eternal death that is a consequence of that fall, an eternal death that he could know as actually occurring in the Crucifixion, where it occurs in that second Adam who is an apocalyptically new Adam, and now it occurs as apocalypse itself. A uniquely Christian apocalypse is inseparable from the Crucifixion, or inseparable from that resurrection which is the consequence of crucifixion, and just as the cross is the purest symbol of Christianity, it is the most offensive symbol in the world, and perhaps most offensive to that Christian world that has so profoundly resisted and reversed the Crucifixion. Primitive Christian Gnosticism arose as a refusal or reversal of the Crucifixion, a Gnosticism that could only know Christ as the Christ of Glory, now crucifixion becomes resurrection and resurrection alone, and if this is a resurrection dissolving every possible apocalyptic horizon, this occurs by way of an ultimately primordial movement.

Gnosticism is that form of Christianity that is most totally directed to an eternal life and glory, but it has a full counterpart in the greater body of Christianity, one that is in quest of eternal life above all else, and one that can primarily know Christ as the giver of that eternal life. Once it was common to interpret Pauline Christianity as the Hellenization of an originally Jewish Christianity, but no Hellenistic mystery cult so centers its life upon death and immortality as does ancient Christianity, and while persecution and martyrdom could understandably issue in such an acceptance of death, nowhere else in history can one discover such a comprehensive and passionate longing for death, a passion that although checked was not reversed by the Constantinian triumph of the Church.

Originally, Christian baptism was an apocalyptic initiation into the new æon, but in the Hellenistic Church it becomes an initiation into eternal life, a life that is continually renewed in the liturgical action of the Eucharist, and an eternal life that is not interrupted by the event of death. Now redemption is eternal peace in the celestial paradise of Christ, a Christ who in the earliest Christian art is the Shepherd of souls and the Teacher of Eternal Life, and after Constantine this early esoteric figure passes into the Teacher of True Wisdom or Gnosis. Nowhere throughout this iconographic tradition is there a suffering or crucified Christ, and it is not until the fifth century after Christ that representations of the Crucifixion occur in Christian art, but then they are virtually shapeless, and it is only after the ending of patristic Christianity in the sixth century that the Crucifixion actually becomes present in Christian art. So, too, the Crucifixion is minimal throughout ancient or patristic theology, at least from the perspective of modern Christianity, for the Crucifixion does not become central or primal in theology until Luther, and even Dante could not envision the crucified Christ. But with the waning of the medieval world, the Crucifixion becomes primal throughout Western Christianity, and if this, too, is an ultimate historical transformation of Christianity, it even thereby is a genuine rebirth of primitive Christianity.

Nothing is more distinctive of a uniquely modern Christianity than its ultimate centering upon the Crucifixion, and just as images of the resurrection move ever more fully into the periphery of Christian art, the Crucifixion becomes all in all, and this is reflected not only in Christian art but in Christian poetry and thinking. If only through the Crucifixion we can understand Hegel as a uniquely Christian thinker, Hegel is the first philosopher to incorporate the Crucifixion into pure thinking, this occurs in his revolutionary kenotic thinking of an absolute self-negation or an absolute self-emptying, a self-emptying and self-negation that is the embodiment of Absolute Spirit. The Crucifixion as an absolutely kenotic movement becomes all in all in Hegel's purely dialectical philosophy, and if this is a renewal of an original Christianity, it is simultaneously a profound transformation of all historical Christianity, and as such it can be understood as a paradigm of a truly new Christianity.

At no point does a uniquely twentieth century imagination more deeply differ from its predecessors than in the ultimacy with which it centers upon death, and for the first time in Western history all symbols of immortality now become alien and unreal, an immortality that has disappeared from the fuller or more actual expressions of a new era, and death for the first time can comprehensively be known as an absolutely alien or an absolutely empty death. Nevertheless, it has enormous power in that very alien emptiness, as now death calls more fully or more comprehensively than it had ever done so since ancient Christianity, but now it calls as death alone rather than as a death issuing in immortality. What we can know as religion in our world is a flight from or a reversal of this new death, a flight most comprehensively occurring in a new orthodox Christianity, a new orthodox Christianity that can know our new world as an embodiment of an eternal death, and that can now realize eternal life only by way of a flight from this new world. Thus orthodox theology can know a truly new imagination as an absolutely alien imagination, and above all so because of its embodiment of an eternal death, an eternal death that is an absolute judgment, and an absolutely final judgment.

Yet Christianity knows an absolute death as the one and only source of redemption, proclaiming that Christ's death inaugurated the new creation, and all humanity is now called to participate in this death as the way of salvation. Death, it is true, is a universal motif in the history of religions, and a universal way of ultimate transformation, but only in Christianity is redemptive death an actual and historical death, and only in those worlds that have come under the impact of Christianity can we discover records of a full and concrete experience of the factuality and finality of death. Once again Buddhism presents an illuminating contrast to Christianity, here one discovers unbelievably complex systems of meditation centering upon death, meditations upon death calling forth the ultimacy of death itself, but here death is a way to a dissolution of the human condition, and thus to the dissolution of pain and suffering. Only Christianity calls for a full experience of an actual death and an actual dying as the way to transfiguration and rebirth, and just as the passion story is the very center of the synoptic gospels, it is a meditation upon that passion that is the deepest and purest Christian meditation. For the first time in history there here occurs an opening to the ultimacy of death, one truly alien to the pre-Christian world, and now for the first time death is known as an ultimate event, and nowhere else in history has humanity known an ultimate life through the all too actual event of death itself.

Thus death is absolute in Christianity as it is in no other tradition; this alone could account for the primacy of the fall in Christianity, a fall that is a total fall because it is inseparable from a new totality of death. This totality of death is also inseparable from what Christianity knows as the new creation, only the ending or death of the old creation makes possible the new creation, and Paul knows that ending as occurring in the Crucifixion, a crucifixion thereby manifest as apocalypse itself. This is the very apocalypse that is renewed in a new Christianity and a new apocalypse, but now death is total as it never is in either primitive or ancient Christianity, a totality of death inaugurated by the very advent of the modern world, and one only consummated in our world. The totality of this death is called forth by the uniquely modern symbol of the death of God, and uniquely modern because here and here alone the death of God is the death of the Godhead, a death that alone can realize an absolute transfiguration, and an absolute transfiguration of totality itself.

Although the death of God is a uniquely Christian symbol, it does not become a total symbol until the full advent of the modern world, only then does it enter either the imagination or pure thinking itself, and only then does it become the primary symbol of a new world. Now the death of God is actually embodied in a new history and a new world, both Blake and Hegel could know the French Revolution as the inauguration of full modernity, a revolution that first historically embodied the death of God, and a revolution that is the ending of all pre-modern history. Of course, both Blake and Hegel came to know that revolution as ultimately reversing itself, but it nevertheless is the very center of modern history, and a center marking the final ending of an old world. That ending is inseparable from an historical realization of the death of God, one that both Blake and Hegel could understand as a repetition and renewal of the Crucifixion, but this renewal universalizes the Crucifixion, and universalizes it in an absolutely new world. Thus full modernity is a truly new modernity only by way of the death of God, and as that modernity evolves the death of God becomes ever more comprehensive in a new consciousness and a new society, a new world which is the first fully secular world in history, and if only thereby a truly universal world.

With the full and final actualization of an ultimate death, all innocence disappears, every possible historical return is ended, transcendence itself does not simply vanish but becomes ultimately alien, and a new and total emptiness or nothingness is everywhere. For the death of God is inseparable from the advent of a truly new and even total nihilism, a truly new desert and abyss, a nihilism that Nietzsche knows as a consequence of Christianity, and a consequence of the uniquely Christian God, that God who alone has made possible and made necessary our ultimate abyss. Can we understand the death of God as the necessary and inevitable consequence of a uniquely Christian history, one possible within no other horizon, yet one inevitable within a Christian horizon? No such revolutionary event appears in any other horizon of history, and no other horizon of consciousness is even open to such a possibility, for only in the Christian world is death itself an absolute event, an absolute event that is the center of history, and an absolute event which is apocalypse itself. Inevitably, this absolutely awesome event has provoked a profound Christian resistance, as can be seen concretely in Christian iconography, for the cross does not become a Christian icon until the end of ancient Christianity, it only all too gradually enters Byzantine and medieval art, not truly becoming central in Christian art until the waning or ending of the medieval world. So, too, the Crucifixion is not central or primal in Christian poetry until the seventeenth century, a primacy making possible a poetic revolution, or certainly an epic revolution in *Paradise Lost*, one which all too significantly is deeply weakened if not reversed in *Paradise Regained*, for with the full realization of the Crucifixion there can be no real vision of any paradise except a paradise lost.

Yet if a vision or an enactment of the Crucifixion inevitably culminates in an enactment of the death of God, is this only a perverse vision of the Crucifixion, one knowing crucifixion apart from resurrection, and therefore knowing the crucified Christ as the Antichrist? Theologians are tempted to make this judgment, but they do not dare to do so, for this is a judgment inseparable from a Gnostic horizon, an horizon knowing crucifixion only as resurrection. No, just as nothing is more unique in Christianity than is the Crucifixion, nothing is more primal here than is crucifixion itself, and even if a Christian crucifixion is inseparable from resurrection, that resurrection is inseparable from the Crucifixion. Nor are enactments of resurrection absent from uniquely modern enactments of the death of God, they are primal in both Blake and Hegel, and primal in Nietzsche, too, but these are uniquely modern enactments of resurrection, and they are at a vast distance from their pre-modern counterparts. So, too, there are visions of resurrection throughout late modern literature and art, but these are resurrections inseparable from an ultimate abyss or an ultimate death or an ultimate nothingness, hence inseparable from a nihilistic horizon that is simply inescapable as a consequence of the death of God.

Nietzsche is not alone in understanding our nihilism as a consequence of Christianity, and certainly nothing comparable to our nihilism is found in any other historical world, is this nihilism then a consequence of a full historical actualization of an absolute death, and of an absolute death that is a uniquely Christian death? And if a uniquely Christian death is a fully apocalyptic death, is that not inevitably a nihilistic death, openly nihilistic in its enactment of the end of the world, and purely nihilistic in its ending of the deepest ground of the world? Once again Paul is deeply illuminating, a Paul who could know a grace occurring in the deepest depths of sin, and only the actualization of that grace unveils that old Adam who is the very embodiment of an eternal death, an eternal death that can be understood as an actual and alien nothingness. Paul knows justification as an absolute justification, a transfiguration of old æon into new æon, or of an old creation into a new creation, and thus a transfiguration inseparable from the full actuality of an eternal death or a fully actual nothingness. Inevitably this transfiguration calls forth a truly new antinomianism, or, at least, an antinomianism from every possible perspective of an "old" law or an "old" creation, now that old law and old creation can be known to be truly void, or truly nothing, an absolute negation that Paul could know as occurring in the Crucifixion. Not only is the absolute grace of Christ inseparable from an absolute judgment, but that judgment occurs independently of a knowledge of that grace, now the ultimate power and authority of an old world are ended, an ending occurring even now, and the world itself is now passing into a final nothingness.

Nothing is more revolutionary in Paul's theological thinking than a calling forth of that nothingness, one that deeply affected Valentinian Gnosticism, and then is reborn in a truly new form in Augustine's revolutionary thinking. Although that nothingness is absent from medieval scholastic thinking, it is reborn with the advent of modernity, but not reborn in pure thinking itself until Schelling and Hegel, a rebirth inseparable from Hegel's realization of the death of God, a thinking first realizing the actual nothingness of every possible beyond. Now an actual nothingness ever more fully undergoes an epiphany throughout the modern world, an actual nothingness fully embodied in our new nihilism, and here, too, Paul can be known as a prophet of our world, the only ancient prophet foreseeing our nihilism, and foreseeing it in knowing and enacting an absolutely old world that is now coming to an end, and coming to an end in the very actuality of the world itself. If Paul is the most purely apocalyptic ancient prophet, he has surely been reborn as such in the modern world, and even reborn in that Nietzsche who is the arch-enemy of Paul, a Nietzsche not only proclaiming the end of history, but proclaiming the advent of that absolutely new grace which is Eternal Recurrence, and an eternal recurrence absolutely voiding everything that stands forth apart from itself as either existence or the world. In knowing Paul as his deepest enemy, Nietzsche could know a mirror image of himself, a reverse image, yes, but a reverse image unveiling the deep continuity between Nietzsche and Paul.

If only through the modern realization of the death of God, we can know the absoluteness of death itself, and know it as it has never been known before, never before has the death of God been so comprehensive or so universal, even a Hegel appears as an innocent in the perspective of the twentieth century. Now an absolute judgment can be realized surpassing even that judgment that Augustine and Luther could know, and it is just by a realization of that judgment that a truly anti-philosophical theology is born, a birth that does not truly occur until the twentieth century, and born in that Barth who could know an ultimate judgment more deeply than any other theologian. Now a truly new absolute death is called forth theologically, and a truly new damnation, and for the first time since the young Luther the crucified Christ can be known as being truly damned, a damnation making impossible the damnation of all others, an ultimate damnation that Barth can know as the consequence of an eternal election or predestination, and a predestination that is the very substance of the Gospel (*Church Dogmatics*, II, 2).

Barth has given us our only truly or fully modern dogmatic theology, and not only is it the most influential theology of the twentieth century, but the most revealing one as well, and most revealing of Christian theology itself, a theology that can finally be a genuine theology only by being a theology of absolute death. If only for this reason, Barth could know philosophical theology, and most clearly scholastic theology, as the very voice of the Antichrist, but an Antichrist only openly manifest in full modernity, when philosophical thinking is inseparable from a thinking of the death of God. But is it only in the horizon of that death that an actual theology of absolute death becomes possible, such a theology is absent throughout the world of Christendom, and Barth is certainly vastly distant from that world in his understanding of election or predestination. And has Paul himself only been fully discovered theologically in modernity, Pauline scholars commonly affirm that Paul has never been understood theologically, and that our first Christian theology is that theology that is most misunderstood, and most misunderstood by our most systematic theologians, whose very systems inevitably dissolve or reverse the revolutionary Paul.

Nevertheless, it is Hegel, our most systematic thinker, who can be understood to have truly recovered Paul, and recovered Paul in his most purely dialectical and kenotic thinking, a thinking making possible Kierkegaard's discovery of faith, a discovery only possible through the end of Christendom, for it is a discovery of that Incarnation that *is* Crucifixion. Kierkegaard is Hegelian and anti-Hegelian simultaneously. He is certainly Hegelian in knowing the uniquely Christian God as the absolutely self-emptied God (*Philosophical Fragments*), a self-emptied God in Incarnation and Crucifixion at once. Here we encounter a truly Kierkegaardian absolute paradox, and an absolute paradox only possible through a pure reversal of both consciousness and history. Surely this is a recovery of Paul, although not a recovery of the apocalyptic Paul, but nevertheless Kierkegaard, too, can be known as a father of nihilism, and a father of nihilism in so deeply knowing and enacting an absolute No, an absolute No that is our purest assault upon philosophy until Nietzsche, and one also paralleling Nietzsche in its ultimate assault upon our deepest interiority. Although wholly beyond Kierkegaard's intention, we can understand such an assault as yet another primal source of our nihilism, one in which our deepest existence becomes absolutely groundless, and we are standing over an ultimate abyss.

From a fully modern perspective, ancient and orthodox Christianity have never truly or fully known the Incarnation, never known an incarnation that is inseparable from crucifixion, or inseparable from a descent into the deepest abyss. Kierkegaard certainly knows that abyss, and knows it in knowing an absolute No, a No that he knows as the No of God, and a No inevitably encountered in a truly deep descent, or in that descent that occurs in a fully modern world. But is that a No that can be known apart from a uniquely modern epiphany of the Christian God, certainly Kafka knows such a No, and knows it with a purity to be discovered nowhere else, could that be a decisive sign of the God of absolute death, and of the universal epiphany of that God? This is the God whom the Christian knows as the ultimate source of the Crucifixion, and therefore the ultimate source of the death of God Himself? Barth surely knows this, although this is disguised by his orthodox theological language, but can a genuinely Christian theological language escape this, has not Christian theology always known God as the ultimate source of the Crucifixion? Although traditional orthodoxy denies that the divinity of Christ dies in the Crucifixion, this is not a real possibility for that Barth who knows the fullness of the Godhead in the sacrifice of Christ, just as it is not a real possibility for any genuinely modern theology. If only at this point, there is a true chasm between a truly modern and a truly ancient theology, and a chasm reflecting an ultimate transformation of Christianity.

The Crucifixion can be understood as an ultimate ending of every possible eternal return, and if ancient Christianity deeply renewed the movement of eternal return, it inevitably thereby either muted or annulled the Crucifixion, an annulment clearly occurring in Gnosticism, but one also occurring in an orthodox Christian understanding of the Godhead. That absolutely transcendent and absolutely primordial Godhead is at the furthest possible point from crucifixion, one most infinitely distant from an absolute death; thus the cross is most offensive to a uniquely Christian consciousness of God, one knowing an absolute transcendence as it had never been known before, and both Kierkegaard and Luther could know the "offense" of faith as being most deeply offensive to the Christian world itself. This is an offense inseparable from an absolute death, the absolute death of the Crucifixion, and while a uniquely Christian interiority has always known that death, Christian dogma has resolutely refused it, or if not refused it, wholly veiled it, and if it is just at this point that Barth is most radical theologically, this is a theological radicalism that is truly a renewal of the New Testament, but one that occurs only after two millennia of theological history. Could this be a confirmation of Kierkegaard's judgment that Christendom has absolutely negated Christ? But this is a judgment that already arises both in the Spiritual Franciscans and in the Radical Reformation, and one that is at least implicitly if not explicitly present in that Jansenism that gave us not only Racine and Pascal but a deep religious underground in France, one that explodes in the French Revolution, a revolution enacting the universality of an absolute death.

Our world vastly differs from the ancient world in its understanding of death. Epicureanism, the most atheistic of all ancient thinking, can be known as a pious thinking from our perspective, and above all so in its thinking of death. Only in the ancient world is a truly innocent death possible, one that becomes impossible after the advent of the Christian world, but most impossible after the advent of the modern world. Only in the Christian world can a thinking of death draw forth an ultimate horror or an ultimate *Angst*, one truly absent in Greek tragedy, but one ever more overwhelming in the evolution of modern tragedy, with the exception of the second part of Goethe's *Faust*, which is our most pagan drama. That is a drama that becomes impossible in late modernity, an historical era obsessed with death, even if one that has most muted death in the public realm, but that very muting is a decisive sign, and a sign of a new terror of death. So, too, it is only in the twentieth century that there is a pure and comprehensive philosophical thinking of death, one most profoundly occurring in Heidegger's *Being and Time*, and if it is Heidegger's thinking that has most deeply confronted a uniquely modern poetry, that is a poetry inseparable from an ultimate enactment of death. Can this be known as a uniquely Christian impact upon our modernity?

If the ancient world is truly innocent from our perspective in its interior enactment of death, thereby we can know an absence of interior depth in that world, an absence that is the absence of that interiority that was born with the advent of Christianity, an interiority first recorded in the epistles of Paul, and there inscribed as an interiority profoundly at war with itself. This is that ultimate conflict between "flesh" and Spirit that Paul knows so deeply, one only released by the Crucifixion, and therefore one inseparable from an absolute death, and an absolute death first making possible an interior experience of death. Now self-consciousness itself is born, a consciousness absent from the ancient world, but it is born only by way of an ultimate experience of death, the death of that "I" that is most deeply my own, and while this occurs in that ultimate judgment released by the Crucifixion, it is that very judgment that makes possible a Christian discovery of that "I" that is only my own, an "I" that is the absolute opposite of the grace of Christ, but an "I" that only appears as an "I" to itself through the ultimate impact of the Crucifixion. This is a truly doubled "I," one absolutely torn between "flesh" and Spirit, and while the "I" of the Spirit is wholly a gift of Christ, an "I" that is only my own is the true opposite of the "I" of the Spirit, so a consciousness is born that is an absolutely polarized or absolutely self-divided consciousness, a birth that is the advent of what we have known as self-consciousness.

That self-consciousness will not be discovered again until Augustine, who philosophically discovered self-consciousness, thereby giving us our first philosophical understanding of "subject," and for Augustine this truly new understanding is possible only as a consequence of the Incarnation. That is an ultimate beginning making possible the birth of a truly new interiority, one wholly absent from the pre-Christian world, or from the pre-Christian pagan world, an interiority ever enlarging and deepening itself in the evolution of Christendom, and one making possible the modern philosophical advent of the "subject" in Descartes, a Descartes who could know himself as an Augustinian. Yet our deepest philosophical Augustinian is Hegel, who is even Augustinian in his understanding of the death of God, and precisely so because of the new and absolute primacy here of subject. Hegel is most explicitly Augustinian in his understanding of the Unhappy Consciousness, or that new form of consciousness that realizes itself only by losing all the essence and substance of itself, but this is an ultimate loss, and far more ultimate than an Augustinian loss of selfhood, and it issues in an absolutely new interior realization that God Himself is dead, an ultimate and absolute death that is the very advent of the "pure subjectivity" of substance itself, and this advent is the inbreathing of the Spirit, one in which Substance actually becomes Subject (*Phenomenology of Spirit*, 785). Is Hegel here recording an actual experience of his own, one of the rare points in his own writing where he echoes the *Confessions*, and if Hegel can be understood to have undergone an ultimate conversion, that is a conversion made possible by this experience, certainly an interior experience of an absolute death, and one now revolutionizing philosophy itself.

Both Augustine and Hegel were philosophical revolutionaries, and revolutionaries in their absolutely new thinking of "subject," but in Hegel as opposed to Augustine that thinking is a thinking of an absolute death, and while each can truly know subject only by way of a self-negation of that subject itself, it is only Hegel who can know an absolute self-negation of God Himself. Here, too, lies a gulf between the ancient and the modern world, but is there an actual possibility of our return to an ancient world, or any real possibility of return at all? Can we truly return from an absolute death, or can we only numb or disguise it, and if postmodernity is the advent of a truly new emptiness, and one now realizing a universalization of an actual emptiness, and a universalization of a new and absolute anonymity, are these universal embodiments of an absolute death, but now embodiments that are wholly exterior rather than interior, and embodiments bringing an end to interiority itself? Could this be a final consequence of Christianity, a Christianity alone knowing an absolute death, and perhaps a Christianity most powerful in that very realization? Or most powerful in our new world?

Chapter Two

Jesus and the Incarnation

The Name of Jesus

Why Jesus? Christianity has always been confronted from both within and without by the primal question of why it makes such an absolute claim for the unique and individual Jesus of Nazareth. Now that Christendom has either perished or become wholly transformed, this question has become more compelling than ever, for if a new universal world has truly been born, how could such a claim be meaningful or real? What can the name of Jesus mean in our new world? Must it inevitably reflect only a limited and an all too particular history and consciousness, one inevitably contracting in a truly new world, so much so that now it can offer only a way into a vanishing or moribund past rather than a way into a genuine future? Is the very name of Jesus actually and fully namable in our time? Is it now possible to pronounce that name in a fully actual moment, or in a moment in which we are truly alive and awake? And if every individual name is now passing into a truly new and comprehensive anonymity, how could this not be true of the name of Jesus? These questions have become so overwhelming that they are seldom asked in the Christian world, or in the manifest Christian world, yet they are inescapable questions for Christianity, and perhaps questions decisively unveiling the deeper pathology of the contemporary Christian world. For the name of Jesus could have become for us a name evoking a deep impotence, or an ultimate passivity, or a tomb enclosing and freezing all energy and life, and certainly so if Christianity has truly undergone an ultimate and final reversal, and a genuine reversal of its original and revolutionary ground.

Modern Biblical scholarship has revolutionized our understanding of the original Jesus, and most clearly so by decisively unveiling the multiple and irreconcilable images of Jesus in the New Testament itself; nothing else has made so fully manifest the truly divergent and conflicting forces of primitive Christianity, or so fully called forth the illusion of an original and orthodox Christianity. The very idea of a New Testament theology as opposed to New Testament theologies is now simply impossible, and nothing is now more challenging to New Testament scholarship than the deeply modern project of discovering the historical Jesus; and even if there is a substantial consensus that this Jesus is an apocalyptic Jesus, we are ever increasingly baffled by what this could possibly mean. While New Testament scholars and theologians are largely agreed that the original Jesus is a truly revolutionary Jesus, there is no agreement at all as to what this revolution actually means, or to what degree it is embodied in the early Christian churches. A dominant paradigm in the twentieth century quest for the historical Jesus is truly revealing, and that is that we can judge a recorded act or saying of Jesus to be historically authentic to the very degree that it is most challenging or most offensive to the primitive churches. We now know that those churches were in deep conflict with each other, and most in conflict over the ultimate question of the very identity of Jesus, which can be understood as the deepest of all questions in Christianity.

Innumerable images and enactments of Jesus can be discovered in Christian history, enactments and images often if not commonly deeply differing from each other. These images and enactments can be understood as a reflection of the New Testament itself; nevertheless, profound transformations of the New Testament Jesus have occurred in Christian history, and perhaps most so when Christianity has been most powerful and most creative. These transformations have occurred in both revolutionary and counterrevolutionary directions, and commonly a revolutionary expression of Jesus has almost immediately been accompanied by its own reversal, as can be seen at all of the great turning points of Christian history. Once again, Christian iconography is revealing, and if that iconography can be understood to have evolved by way of an organic and even necessary evolution, it is all too significant that images of Jesus have virtually disappeared in the major expressions of twentieth century art, or, if not disappeared, have become wholly anonymous. So, too, we can discover an evolution of Jesus in a uniquely Christian epic, and if this begins with Dante, Dante's Jesus is wholly and only the Christ of Glory, but in Milton Jesus is the Christ of Glory and the Christ of Passion at once, and in Blake Jesus is only and wholly the Christ of Passion. Our epic Jesus also evolves insofar as he becomes ever more fully and finally the apocalyptic Jesus, and if there is a genuine parallel to this in Christian painting, that could illuminate the anonymity of Jesus in the twentieth century imagination, for a finally apocalyptic Jesus is a Jesus who is all in all.

The apocalyptic Jesus is the most revolutionary Jesus in Christian history. This alone could account for the fact that this Jesus was not historically discovered until after almost two millennia of Christian history, and if it is orthodox Christianity that most subverts the apocalyptic Jesus, it is radical Christianity that most fully embodies him, and embodies Jesus as an ultimately revolutionary power. This is all too clear both in the Radical Reformation and in the English Revolution, but it is also clear in our most revolutionary thinking and vision, as witness Hegel and Blake. No philosopher is so deeply bound to Jesus as is Hegel, just as no poet is so Christocentric as is Blake, and Blake and Hegel share a profoundly and a uniquely Christocentric movement, the purely kenotic movement of an absolute self-negation or self-emptying, a kenotic movement that becomes total in both Hegel and Blake. Moreover, this is an ultimately apocalyptic movement in Hegel and Blake alike, and just as Blake is our first purely apocalyptic poet, Hegel is our first purely apocalyptic philosopher; thereby, an original Christian apocalypse is reborn in full modernity, but reborn only by way of an apocalyptic realization of the death of God. Both Blake and Hegel know that apocalyptic death as occurring in that Incarnation that culminates in Crucifixion, just as both know that the only resurrection then possible is absolute apocalypse itself.

Now it is truly remarkable that it is only a secularized world that called forth such vision and thinking, one never possible in the world of Christendom, and one a universe removed from the world of the Church. And if thereby we have been given a fully revolutionary Jesus who is a purely apocalyptic Jesus, can this all too modern Jesus be understood as a genuine renewal of the original Jesus of Nazareth? Of course, this could be true only if Jesus had truly been annulled, or forgotten, or reversed in the course of Christian history; hence Blake could know the Christ of the Church as the dead body in the tomb, a truly radical image of the dominant Christ of the Church that is found throughout radical Christianity, a Christianity that could know Jesus only by negating the Christ of the Church. Something fully parallel to this is found throughout the greater body of New Testament scholarship, and above all so in the second half of the twentieth century, and if this gave birth to a uniquely modern fundamentalism, this fundamentalism has unveiled a Christianity that can be Christian only by dissolving all critical scholarship and critical thinking. While this is the only form of Christianity that vast numbers of people now know, is this yet another expression of our forgetting of Jesus, and is Jesus most deeply forgotten when he is most openly affirmed?

Is it possible truly to forget Jesus? Is this a name that can actually disappear, or is this a name that is inevitably renewed, even if this should occur by way of a transformation of the original Jesus? Blake could understand Jesus as the "Universal Humanity," a Jesus who is present in every voice and face, and most immediately present in our deepest suffering and joy. And Blake could continually affirm this in a world that he believed had ceased to be Christian, a world that is a truly apocalyptic darkness, and he could know Jesus as the very center of this darkness, although a center absolutely reversing darkness itself. Thus it is Blake who gives us our first full vision of Jesus' descent into Hell, a Hell that is truly our own, and yet a Hell that even now is being transfigured into an apocalyptic Heaven. This is nothing less than an absolute transfiguration, and an absolutely total transfiguration, one which for Blake is inseparable from the name of Jesus, so that he can give the motto "only Jesus" to his greatest work, *Jerusalem*, a work that can be understood as the first full expression of our final apocalyptic vision. Thereby it is a genuine counterpart to Hegel's *Phenomenology of Spirit*, and perhaps to his *Science of Logic* as well, and Hegel's purely dialectical thinking no less revolves about an absolute transfiguration, one fully paralleling the apocalyptic transfiguration that Blake envisioned, and one no less grounded in the name of Jesus, even if that name is now named as absolute negativity itself.

A decisive clue to a uniquely Hegelian negativity is the word *kenosis* itself, a word appearing not only at many of the most decisive points of the *Phenomenology*, but a word unveiling as no other word does the whole movement of Hegel's thinking, a movement that is nothing less than an absolute self-negation, and a self-negation that the *Science of Logic* can know as an absolute self-emptying. There is only one actual name that can be associated with that self-emptying, and that is the name of Jesus, a Jesus who is the very paradigm of an absolute and an actual self-emptying, and not only the Jesus who is the sacrificial Victim, but the Jesus who actually enacted the dawning of the Kingdom of God, a dawning that both Blake and Hegel understand as the self-negation of a heavenly transcendence, one absolutely transfiguring that transcendence, so that transcendence itself is now only here and now. That is the total presence that is here evoked by the name of Jesus or its counterpart, but a total presence that is an absolutely self-emptying or self-negating presence, hence a presence that is a totally sacrificial presence, and that is the very presence that we inevitably name as Jesus. If this is the naming that is our deepest naming, it need not be confined to the literal name of Jesus, but it is inseparable from the actual act of naming, and is so even when that naming is silent, for naming is our primary way of recognition, a recognition that is finally a recalling of our deepest summons and call.

That is the recalling evoked by the name of Jesus, but as opposed to the name of the Buddha, this is not a name recalling a primordial absolute emptiness, but rather one recalling or renewing the absolute act of incarnation itself, an incarnation releasing an ultimate and final actuality. Hence this is the movement that is reversed by the Christian movement of eternal return, just as it is annulled by that uniquely Christian God who is absolute sovereignty and absolute transcendence alone, a God who can be known only as the absolutely majestic Creator, and never as the absolutely kenotic and sacrificial Servant. While Christology knows Christ as Lord and Servant at once, orthodox Christology knows the Servant only as the humanity of Christ, so that it is only that humanity that suffers and dies in the Crucifixion. Aquinas could speak for the ancient Christian tradition as a whole in declaring that Christ's passion did not concern or affect his Godhead, for God's nature eternally remains impassible, and can neither be wounded nor suffer any change, so Christ suffered only in his "lower powers," and Christ's soul suffered only insofar as it was allied with the body of Jesus (*Summa Theologica* III, 46, 8-12). Here, the body of Jesus is clearly not the Godhead of Christ, for Godhead is eternal and can never suffer or die, hence the orthodox condemnation of Patripassionism, which is nothing less than a condemnation of a total incarnation, an incarnation in which Godhead itself becomes wholly and finally incarnate.

Certainly orthodox Christology is a refusal of a total Incarnation, just as it is a refusal of the Word made "flesh." Here, the union between the humanity and the deity of Christ is one occurring only in the Christ of Glory, and never in the Christ of Passion, a passion absolutely alien to Godhead itself, just as the death of God is absolutely alien to that Godhead. Both ancient and medieval Christianity know the Incarnation as realizing the deification of humanity, or the deification of a humanity eternally predestined to redemption, and while the Reformation was an assault upon this deification, this is a deification only fully dissolved with the full advent of the modern world, an advent inevitably ending Christendom. Just as Christendom can know the Godhead of Jesus as the very way to eternal life, this is the Godhead of the Christ of Glory alone, and every full realization of the Christ of Passion has been a reversal of that Christ of Glory who is the way to eternal life, one not only knowing the ultimacy of suffering and death, but knowing that death and suffering as occurring in the fullness and the totality of Christ. Nothing could be more heretical or heterodox to orthodox Christianity, hence the Christ of Passion and the orthodox Christ are in ultimate opposition, and most clearly so in the ultimate dichotomy between the Christ of Passion and the Christ of Glory. Only with the ending of Christendom can the Christ of Passion be known as the fullness of Godhead itself, and only then is it possible to know the absolute self-emptying or the absolute sacrifice of the Godhead, a sacrifice that is not only the sacrifice of the Crucifixion, but the sacrifice or the self-emptying of the Incarnation, too.

The radical or revolutionary Christian evokes that incarnation by the very name of Jesus. Here this name is truly unique, and truly unique as it could never be in orthodox Christianity, for orthodox Christianity in knowing Jesus as the Christ of Glory shares this knowledge of a redeemer with a vast body of religion both East and West, whereas the Christ who is the Christ of Passion is known by Christianity alone, and surely not known by those mystery cults that cannot know a total and final incarnation. Christianity also knows an ultimacy of naming itself, which is genuinely unique, for while this occurs in Judaism, there the pronunciation of the name of God is deeply forbidden, whereas the Christian knows himself or herself as Christian by the very pronunciation of the name of Jesus, a pronunciation that is the center of both Christian worship and Christian witness. And that witness and worship is least Christian, or least uniquely Christian, when it evokes the name of Jesus apart from an ultimate movement of incarnation, or apart from crucifixion, for the Christ who is worshipped only as the Christ of Glory is not only inseparable from archaic religion, but inseparable from the archaic movement of eternal return, or inseparable from a movement of return to an absolutely primordial Godhead.

Already Paul celebrates the Crucifixion as apocalypse itself, and while Paul does not employ the language of incarnation, except in his hymn to the kenotic Christ (Philippians 2:5-11), Paul nevertheless deeply knows the Incarnation in knowing the ultimacy of the Crucifixion, an ultimacy so great as to remove almost all of Paul's attention from Jesus of Nazareth, for Paul fully knows Jesus only as the Crucified, which is

surely Paul's deepest name of Jesus. In the synoptic gospels, the crucifixion of Jesus wholly overshadows his resurrection, and so much so that
here the resurrection stories are not only inconsistent with each other,
but in themselves pale into virtual insignificance in the perspective of
the passion story, a profound imbalance that is transformed by the
Fourth Gospel, and the Fourth Gospel is the only ancient writing that
truly integrates incarnation, crucifixion, resurrection, and apocalypse.
Yet the Fourth Gospel is the only canonical gospel that can know Jesus
as Lord, or fully know Jesus as Lord, here truly paralleling the Gnostic
Gospel of Thomas, but in the fourth gospel Jesus is incarnate Lord,
and hence undergoes a suffering and death impossible for a Gnostic
deity. And impossible for every pre-Christian apprehension of Godhead
itself, so Jesus is most uniquely the name of that suffering and death,
an ultimate death finally inseparable from the Incarnation itself. Thus
if Jesus is the name of the Incarnation, and of a once and for all and
absolutely unique incarnation, that incarnation finally realizes itself
as absolute death, and only that death makes possible or actualizes a
uniquely Christian resurrection.

Christianity evolves in the ancient world only by reversing both
Paul and the canonical gospels, and it does so by ever more fully sub-
ordinating crucifixion to resurrection, one manifest in the evolution
of ancient Christian liturgy, iconography, and theology, and one
completed in the Constantinian establishment of the Church. Now
the name of Jesus is only actually the name of Lord, and an absolutely
sovereign and transcendent Lord, and if Arianism posed the deepest
theological challenge to Constantinian Christianity, this is clearly a
challenge to Christ the Lord of orthodox Christianity, a Lord that
Arianism could know as being truly divorced from Jesus. Is it actually
possible to name the Christ of Glory as Jesus, or as Jesus of Nazareth,
or as Jesus the Servant and Victim? True, Augustine will not refuse the
kenotic Christ, although his deep NeoPlatonism continually threatens
if it does not embody such a refusal, and if Augustine names Jesus
more fully and more continually than any other ancient theologian,
this is a Jesus inseparable not only from an apocalyptic redemption

but also from an apocalyptic judgment, a judgment inducing the most ultimate guilt recorded in the ancient world. Certainly Jesus the Judge is inseparable from that guilt, a guilt impossible apart from Jesus, or a guilt impossible in consciousness itself apart from Jesus, an absolutely guilty consciousness that is an ultimate consequence of the Incarnation.

Thus if the name of Jesus is inseparable from an absolute apocalypse, it is also inseparable from an absolute fall, or from a realization, and an interior realization, of that fall. Both an interior self-consciousness and an absolute fall are first recorded in the writing of Paul, and if Augustine is the first truly Pauline theologian, he clearly is so in his calling forth of a wholly interior guilt, a guilt assuaged only by Christ, and only in that Jesus whom Augustine knows as Christ. The Augustinian Christ is absolute grace and absolute judgment at once, a grace impossible apart from that judgment, hence a grace realizable only in the depths of guilt, a guilt that is not known until after the Incarnation, and thus not known apart from the incarnate Lord. So it is that an ultimate guilt is here inseparable from the name of Jesus, and the Christ of Glory inseparable from an absolute and apocalyptic judgment, for Augustine is not only a Pauline theologian but also and even thereby an apocalyptic theologian, an apocalyptic ground making possible his creation of the theology of history. *The City of God* is Augustine's most revolutionary work, and even if it profoundly transforms an original Christian apocalypticism, it nevertheless renews it, and renews it most purely theologically by comprehensively enacting a *felix culpa* or fortunate fall, a fall necessarily and comprehensively issuing in that apocalypse that is absolute judgment and absolute redemption at once, and an apocalypse only possible by way of God's eternal act of predestination.

For the first time, Jesus is now understood not only as the center of history, but as the ultimate actor in history itself, and while Augustine continually and prayerfully gives this title to God alone, it is the Son of God who actually acts in history, and just as all of the power of the Father resides in the Son, that power is actualized in history through the

Son. Every historical event whatsoever occurs through his providence, a providence both of judgment and of grace, and a providence that will historically be all in all in the apocalypse. It is seldom noted that only once does Augustine here identify the City of God with the Catholic Church (XX, 9), and even if there is an absolute dichotomy between the City of God and the City of Man, this is a dichotomy that is realized in the fullness of history, and therein realized through Jesus himself, that Son of God who here for the first time is comprehensively known as the Lord of history. Thus Augustine can understand the name of Jesus as the name of the totality of history, a history evolving from fall to apocalypse, for history only begins with the fall, a fall creating that absolute dichotomy that will culminate in absolute apocalypse.

A uniquely modern understanding of history can be and has been understood as a secularization of the *City of God*, a secularization in which the City of Man becomes all in all, but does history therein become less apocalyptic or less total? Not until Augustine is the totality of history drawn forth in thinking itself, a thinking that Augustine knew as only being possible through Christ, hence only possible through the name of Jesus itself, that name of names that has named every name that occurs in history, even if that naming is an absolute judgment. Yet the absolute judgment of Christ is inseparable from the absolute grace of Christ, so that the absolute No of Jesus is inseparable from his absolute Yes, and therefore the name of Jesus here simultaneously evokes an absolute Yes and an absolute No. Do we, too, evoke that name in knowing an absolute No that is an absolute Yes, or in realizing an absolute judgment that is an absolute grace, or an absolute grace that is an absolute ending? If an apocalyptic judgment is now all in all, is that possible apart from an apocalyptic grace, or possible apart from what our history has known as Jesus? Is that history necessary and essential to what we have come to know as the totality of history, and is it possible to name that totality apart from naming Jesus, or apart from naming that absolute Yes and that absolute No that he embodied?

Is it possible that there is a name of Jesus that is now uniquely our own, one only possible and actual in our world, but one nevertheless in continuity both with the original Jesus of Nazareth and with the renaming and renewals of Jesus in our history, renewals that again and again have had a revolutionary historical impact, even if these are seemingly reversed in our world? The very paradigm of reversal could be a decisive model here, and just as radical thinkers and visionaries have understood Christianity itself as a reversal of Jesus, is it possible that a reversal of this reversal could be a renewal of Jesus? And is such a reversal even possible apart from the name of Jesus, or apart from the history actualized by that name, or apart from a consciousness ultimately grounded in Jesus? Is it simply an accident, and a destructive one at that, that we inevitably know history as being centered in Jesus, inevitably know history as either before or after Christ, and thus know Jesus as the one absolute dividing line in history, and one apart from which history loses all meaning? Or has history now inevitably lost all real or ultimate meaning, and is this a deep source of our nihilism, a nihilism unique in history, and one that is an inevitable consequence of Christianity itself? Nietzsche again and again proclaimed the Christian origin of our nihilism, and his very discovery of a uniquely modern nihilism culminated in *The Antichrist*. Here he can know the uniquely Christian God as the very deification of nothingness (18), and perhaps this alone makes possible his unveiling of the gospel of Jesus as the very opposite of the gospel or *dysangel* of Christianity (39). No thinker so deeply centered his thinking upon reversal as did Nietzsche, unless this is true of Hegel himself, but Hegel and Nietzsche are those primal thinkers who think most fully about Jesus, and if they have given us our most ultimate and comprehensive thinking of reversal, perhaps that is a thinking inseparable from the name of Jesus.

Self-Emptying

There is no full thinking or actual vision of self-emptying, or of a total self-emptying, until the full advent of the modern world. Only then do kenotic Christologies appear in Christianity, and these occur only after the uniquely modern realization of the death of God. If Hegel is our most purely kenotic thinker, and Blake our most purely kenotic poet, this is a thinking and a vision only possible by way of an absolute negation of Godhead itself, or certainly a negation of every given or manifest God. Both Blake and Hegel know *kenosis*, or an absolute self-emptying, as occurring at the very center of both consciousness and history; hence, self-emptying or "self-annihilation" is actuality itself, one that Hegel could know as *Wirklichkeit* and Blake as "Experience," and just as "Experience" is the contrary or the opposite of "Innocence," *Wirklichkeit* or actuality is the contrary or the opposite of passivity or quiescence or inactuality. Hegel can know self-emptying as absolute origin itself, one that is comprehensively enacted in the *Science of Logic*, as absolute Spirit evolves from pure immediacy to total actuality, an evolution that is the movement of absolute "Idea" or "Notion," and a movement that is the consequence of *Trieb*, a *Trieb* or primal urge that is the innermost center of absolute Spirit. In the *Phenomenology of Spirit*, *Trieb* is explicitly *kenosis*, a self-emptying that is the "externalization" of Spirit itself, and it is in the very depths of history and consciousness that Spirit abandons the form of substance and becomes "subject," a subject that itself is ultimately an absolute self-emptying, and that finally realizes itself in the death of God.

Is it possible that this is a genuine understanding of the Crucifixion, and thereby of that Incarnation that is inseparable from Crucifixion, or of what the Christian knows most deeply as Jesus? If so, here Jesus is the "Lord" of history only as an ultimately self-emptying or self-negating power, and Jesus is actual in consciousness itself only as that self-emptying, a self-emptying that is finally the embodiment of Godhead itself. An Hegelian self-embodiment is an ultimate self-emptying or self-negation, and a Blakean "self-annihilation" is that movement, too, and in both Blake and Hegel this most deeply and most ultimately occurs in Godhead itself, an absolute self-emptying that we can know only as the death of God. Hegel can be understood as a radically modern or even an inverted Aristotelian, and most clearly so theologically in his pure dissolution of the mystery of God, but this mystery ends in Blake, too, who thereby not only renews Dante and Milton, but also that Paul who, in the final doxology of the Epistle to the Romans, could declare that the revelation of the mystery that was kept secret for long ages is now disclosed.

Hence we have the paradox that here the death of God is the disclosure of the ultimate mystery of God, or the actual realization of that death is a realization of Godhead itself, or of that Godhead that is most truly actual and real. Even more paradoxically, it is a realization of the death or the absolute self-emptying of God that calls forth the totality of God as it had never been manifest before, a totality of God that is truly all in all, and one that can be identified with actuality itself. Just as the Buddhist can know *Sunyata* as being all in all, and the Hindu can know Brahman-Atman as being all in all, the Blakean or the Hegelian can know the Godhead as being all in all, but only insofar as Godhead itself is an absolute self-emptying or an absolute self-negation. No such Godhead is manifest in the world of Christendom, but Christendom cannot know a Godhead that is all in all, except for its deeply heretical mystical expressions, and these know that Godhead only as an absolutely primordial Godhead, or a Godhead absolutely preceding both history and the world. Not until the end of Christendom can the West know a Godhead that is all in all in both consciousness and the world, and if this already occurs in Spinoza, it only becomes comprehensive in the fullness of the modern world, only then was either a Blake or a Hegel possible, and all too significantly both Hegel and Blake could ecstatically greet their new world as the advent of the final age of the Spirit.

While Blake and Hegel can know the death of God as realizing an ultimate collapse or ending, and as truly shattering the deepest ground of all interiority or self-consciousness, it nevertheless is an absolutely positive event, one not only making possible, but itself embodying the final age of the Spirit, an age in which everything whatsoever will not only be reconciled with each other, but fully integrated with each other, an integration that is the consequence of an absolute transfiguration of the Godhead. That transfiguration can occur only through

the death of God, or the death of the absolutely sovereign and transcendent God, a God whom Blake could name as Satan, and Hegel
could know as abstract Spirit or the "Bad Infinite," and each could
know this God as a consequence of the birth of Christianity, when
for the first time it was possible to know the absolutely transcendent
God. That God only appears and is real in consciousness with the occurrence of the Incarnation, an incarnation ending the beyondness of
the beyond, and it is only an emptied beyondness that can appear and
be real as absolute transcendence and absolute transcendence alone,
a truly alien and empty transcendence that itself is a consequence
of the Incarnation. So the Incarnation itself is a self-emptying of an
absolute transcendence, or the self-emptying of God, and only as a
consequence of that self-emptying is a truly alien and infinitely distant
transcendence actually born, one genuinely absent both from Israel
and the pre-Christian world.

So it is that a comprehensive other-worldliness only dawns in the
West with the advent of Christianity. Only then does there occur a
deep longing for death, for only death makes possible a genuine escape from a wholly fallen world, or a genuine or full transition to the
beyond. However, this is a truly new beyond, one never actually or
fully manifest before, and now Jesus himself is named as the only way
to that beyond. This is the very Jesus whom Blake and Hegel reverse,
hence both give us revolutionary understandings of Jesus, and while
Blake's is a purely imaginative Jesus, Hegel's is a purely conceptual one,
and most decisively so in Hegel's revolutionary understanding of an
absolute negativity. How is it possible to understand Hegel's absolute
negativity as a purely conceptual realization of Jesus, or how is it possible to think that there could be a truly conceptual actualization of
Jesus, one that certainly never occurs in Christendom, and is seemingly alien to thinking itself? This is possible, of course, only if Jesus
can truly be understood as embodying an absolute self-emptying, an
embodiment that truly *is* Jesus, and is not only Jesus of Nazareth but
is the Jesus of the deepest Christian life, or that Jesus who is the way,
the truth, and the life. Not until Hegel was there even an attempt to

conceptually understand that truth, but not until Hegel are we given our first truly post-classical logic, or a thinking that is not only a post-classical thinking but a thinking revolving about and profoundly grounded in the uniquely Christian movements of incarnation, crucifixion, and resurrection or apocalypse.

Whereas Blake arises out of a genuinely Christian epic tradition, one that deeply grounded his own work and vision, there is no Christian philosophical tradition that precedes or grounds Hegel's thinking, or none apart from Augustine's philosophical thinking, the only explicitly Christian philosophical thinking that deeply affected Hegel. Hegel's unique philosophical thinking appears out of an ultimate crisis in philosophical thinking, and yet Hegel virtually created the history of philosophy, understanding his own thinking as the consummation of that history, and a consummation in that every actual expression of that thinking is now fulfilled, and fulfilled in the advent of absolute philosophy itself. But this absolute philosophy is absolutely inseparable from what the Christian knows as incarnation, crucifixion, and apocalypse, thereby it is the most explicitly Christian of all philosophies, and the first philosophy ever to give us full philosophical realizations of these uniquely Christian categories. Once again a deep paradox — can the "atheistic" Hegel be our purest Christian philosopher? The "atheistic" Blake can be and has been known as our most purely Christian fully modern poet, and Blake, too, incorporates the uniquely Christian movements of incarnation, crucifixion, and apocalypse in his prophetic and apocalyptic poetry, and here, too, these movements are inseparable from an ultimate death of God.

In both Blake and Hegel, that death is not simply and only death, but far rather an ultimate and final self-negation and self-emptying, a self-emptying that is the emptying of Godhead itself, and that nonetheless occurs in the full actuality of history and consciousness, a self-emptying that Blake explicitly names as Jesus. Why then is it not possible to recognize an Hegelian self-emptying or absolute negativity as a purely conceptual expression of that Jesus? And what could Hegel possibly mean by the resurrection of God if this is not a resurrection inseparable from the resurrection of Jesus? Resurrection is perhaps the most elusive of all Christian theological categories, the one most transformed by regressions to paganism or pre-Christian categories, and if it is only in full modernity that the theologian has even attempted to divorce a uniquely Christian resurrection from a pre-Christian immortality, it is only in that modernity that it has been possible to recognize the ultimate elusiveness or mystery of resurrection itself. We need not doubt that the resurrection of Jesus is at the very center of an original Christianity, but we have every reason to question what that could possibly mean, just as there are overwhelming historical reasons for thinking that this resurrection was profoundly transformed in subsequent Christian history, and already in the New Testament itself there are deeply different images and enactments of that resurrection, so much so that it is now impossible to reconcile these with each other.

A dialectical principle illuminates this quandary, and that is that the deepest negation embodies the deepest affirmation, or the deepest death is ultimately the deepest life, or the deepest darkness finally the most ecstatic light. Just as the Christian has always known that the resurrection of Jesus is inseparable from the crucifixion of Jesus, a dialectical identity fully enacted in Holy Week or the Pascal liturgy, and even in the Eucharist itself, so it is that resurrection is here the realization of an eternal death, so that a uniquely Christian eternal life is inseparable from a uniquely Christian eternal death. This is just the life that was so profoundly transformed by ancient and medieval Christianity, as witness Christian iconography itself, a transformation that can be understood as a forgetting of Jesus, or a forgetting of the self-emptying Jesus, and a forgetting so deep that only a revolutionary breakthrough could recover or renew it. The truth is that the category of resurrection is ultimate for both Blake and Hegel, but now its realization is so vastly distant from all its counterparts in a manifest or open Christianity that it will not appear to be resurrection at all, and surely not a resurrection that could be known as a Christian resurrection. Hegel is most immediately challenging here, and is so in speaking again and again of the resurrection of God, must that be a truly meaningless language, or is it an authentic recovery of a uniquely Christian resurrection?

Although Hegel never systematically draws forth the meaning of this resurrection, it is clear that here the resurrected God is an absolutely transfigured God, a God who is a pure and total immanence as opposed to a pure and total transcendence, and a resurrected God only possible and real as the consequence of an ultimate death of God. Only an absolute self-emptying of God makes possible the resurrection of God, but that resurrection is the consequence of that self-emptying, and this is a truly apocalyptic resurrection, one giving birth to an absolutely new world. At all of these points this understanding of resurrection is vastly distant from all understanding of either resurrection or immortality in the pre-Christian world, but is it a recovery of a uniquely Christian understanding of resurrection, and a recovery absent from all of our manifest theological worlds? We might note that if a truly Christian resurrection is a truly unique resurrection, just as a truly Christian incarnation is a truly unique incarnation, then inevitably it will be deeply resisted by those who receive it, just as it will, inevitably, be associated with its pre-Christian counterparts. This is just the pattern that we can observe in the New Testament itself, and most clearly in Paul, as in Paul's ecstatic celebration of resurrection in I Corinthians 15, which not only abandons the Crucified Christ who had been at the center of this letter, but which openly employs a purely pagan language of immortality, and one clearly reversing the uniquely Christian meaning of resurrection.

If not even Paul could capture this meaning, or could not do so in his most open language about resurrection, is that an actual possibility for any thinker or visionary, or an actual possibility in the modern world? It is common to speak of the impossibility of understanding Paul, but can we not speak of Paul's own misunderstanding of that which he had most deeply received, a misunderstanding surely inevitable in our first theologian, and above all inevitable if the original Jesus is an ultimately revolutionary Jesus? And is it not true that genuine renewals of Paul are genuine re-creations or transformations of Paul, as clearly occurred in Augustine and Luther, and perhaps have occurred in Blake and Hegel, so that such a renewal of Paul is inevitably a deep transformation of Paul, and the deeper the renewal the deeper the transformation? Hegel can be understood as our most profoundly Pauline modern thinker, and above all so in his centering upon crucifixion and apocalypse, but can he be understood as being more purely Christian than was Paul himself in his understanding of resurrection? Of course, just as Paul often regressed to a pre-Pauline language, Hegel often regressed to a pre-Hegelian language, and particularly so in his university lectures, although we must remember that he neither edited nor published these himself. But, is Hegel's own purely philosophical language a genuine recovery and renewal of a uniquely Christian resurrection?

Hegel is the most systematic thinker of the West, and the only major Western thinker who has created a total system, and that is the very context in which we must understand an Hegelian resurrection, a resurrection inseparable from what the Christian knows as creation, fall, atonement, and apocalypse. For an Hegelian resurrection is a total resurrection, one embodying all of these deeply Christian categories, and one inseparable from that totality of God that Hegel was the first Christian thinker to realize, or the first one truly liberated from a pre-Christian horizon. Here, resurrection itself is the resurrection of the totality of God, and a resurrection only made possible by an absolute self-emptying of the Godhead, a resurrection absolutely transfiguring or even reversing the Godhead, as manifest in the total transfiguration of an absolute transcendence into an absolute immanence. So, too, here resurrection cannot possibly be an individual resurrection, or a resurrection independent of the total transfiguration of all and everything, or a resurrection that is not an absolutely new totality. Not only is resurrection apocalypse itself, but it has no meaning or reality apart from an absolute or total apocalypse, and thus no genuine meaning within a pre-apocalyptic horizon. Hence, resurrection, or a uniquely Christian resurrection, is not only an apocalyptic resurrection, but also a total resurrection, and thus one comprehending everything that we can possibly know as God.

Clearly this is a resurrection that Christian theology has refused, a refusal beginning with Paul, or with Paul's most explicit language about resurrection, but one that has deepened or become ever more comprehensive in subsequent Christian language, and certainly so in all orthodox Christian language. This is a language refusing everything that Hegel could know as an absolute self-emptying, but is it a language precisely thereby refusing a uniquely Christian resurrection, and refusing it if only by way of remaining within the horizon of a pre-Christian understanding of God? Surely that is a horizon making impossible an absolute self-emptying or self-negation, but does it not thereby make impossible what the Christian knows as the absolute event of the Crucifixion, just as it makes impossible an incarnation that is the full and final incarnation of God? Now just as Hegel is the first thinker to realize a purely conceptual understanding of incarnation and crucifixion, thereby finally dissolving the ultimate scholastic distinction between reason and revelation, does he give us a truly conceptual understanding of resurrection, too? As opposed to his comprehensive understanding of incarnation and crucifixion, Hegel never systematically draws forth the meaning of resurrection, but could that be because resurrection is the very horizon of an absolutely new thinking, and thus is only meaningful as that horizon itself?

Once again, Blake can illuminate Hegel, for Blake finally envisions an apocalyptic Body of the Godhead, a body that he names and enacts as the New Jerusalem, and that body is a total resurrection of totality itself, but one occurring only as the consequence of an absolute "Self-Annihilation," a self-annihilation occurring throughout the totality of history itself, and one that Blake again and again names as Jesus. Most startling of all, this resurrection realizes an apocalyptic *coincidentia oppositorum* between Christ and Satan, a Satan who is now fully manifest as God the Creator and Judge, as explicitly envisioned on the penultimate plate of *Jerusalem. Jerusalem* is the most purely apocalyptic embodiment of a uniquely modern imagination, one that is an enactment of a total resurrection, and a resurrection centered in the resurrection of Godhead itself. Yet it is a resurrection only possible as the consequence of an absolute death of the Godhead, only that absolute death makes possible a total resurrection, and only thereby is it possible for us to envision a total resurrection. Hence it can be understood as the consequence of an absolute self-emptying, and even an absolute self-emptying in a uniquely Hegelian sense, for Blake was the first to envision an apocalyptic totality, or a purely apocalyptic totality, just as Hegel was the first to realize a purely apocalyptic understanding of totality itself.

There is a full juxtaposition here between an apocalyptic totality and an absolute and total self-emptying. Only the most ultimate and absolute negation can realize that apocalyptic totality, but this negation is a self-negation or a self-emptying, and only thereby can it make possible an absolutely new totality. Only this totality is a truly resurrected body, so here the resurrected body is a resurrected totality, and a resurrected body only possible as a consequence of an absolute self-emptying. Every understanding and vision of an individual resurrection is a betrayal or a withdrawal from that resurrected body, one that is a renewal of that individual and interior center that perishes in crucifixion. Hence, it is a refusal of crucifixion itself, a refusal comprehensively enacted throughout Christianity. So, too, a refusal of the crucifixion as the crucifixion of God is the refusal of an absolute self-emptying, and inevitably thereby a renewal of that Godhead that perishes in crucifixion. Yet this renewal is not and cannot be the renewal of the pre-crucified God, or not if the Crucifixion is an absolute and total event; it can only be a renewal that is a truly new birth, the birth of a Godhead infinitely distant from the Crucifixion, and therefore that absolutely sovereign and transcendent God that Blake can know as Satan. This is that "Bad Infinite" or purely abstract Spirit that Hegel knows, one that is only possible upon a Christian horizon, and a Christian horizon arising from a reversal of the Crucifixion. Only now is a heaven born that is an absolutely other-worldly heaven, and only now is a resurrection possible that is only a spiritual resurrection, or a resurrection whose only destiny is the beyond.

This is the resurrection that both Blake and Hegel reverse, thereby they call forth a total resurrection, and a total resurrection here and now. Yet this resurrection is possible only as a consequence of the Crucifixion, or as the consequence of a total Incarnation, an incarnation that Hegel could know as finally ending every beyond, or finally ending every Godhead that is beyond. So it is that Hegel conjoins and unites Incarnation and Crucifixion, for the Incarnation itself is an absolute self-emptying of the Godhead, or the self-emptying of every Godhead that is beyond. Even Heidegger can recognize that it is Hegel who first ended metaphysics itself, a metaphysics that comprehensively perishes or is reversed in the *Science of Logic*, but that is inevitably ended by a realization of the death of God, a death finally ending everything that the West has known as either Being or God. But Hegel knows this death as a consequence of the Incarnation, as a consequence of the self-emptying of the Godhead, a self-emptying that only becomes fully actual in the Incarnation, an incarnation absolutely transforming both history and consciousness, a transformation which is finally resurrection itself. Already both Paul and the Gospel of John can know that crucifixion which is resurrection, an identity truly lost in the great body of Christianity, and surely lost in Christian theology even if not lost in a uniquely Christian liturgy, but this is the resurrection that both Blake and Hegel truly renew.

We must not imagine that either Blake or Hegel are truly isolated or alone; each can be understood as inaugurators of a full modernity, and whose impact has therein been greater than that of any other fully modern poets or thinkers. Hegel can be and has been understood as the Aristotle of our world, its only fully systematic and comprehensive thinker, and a thinker with whom every subsequent thinker must deeply contend. And irony of ironies, our world may thereby be understood as a truly Christian world, even if this is possible only by a total transformation of Christianity, a transformation that both Blake and Hegel call forth. Twentieth century historiography has called forth a fully comparable transformation that occurred during the first century of Christianity, even as it has made manifest a truly parallel transformation of Israel issuing in the birth of Judaism in the first exile, and if these are ultimate transformations, they can make possible an understanding of an ultimate transformation of Christianity that is occurring in our world. But it is our theology that is most closed to such a transformation, and above all a contemporary theology that is resolutely refusing the absolutely new, and if only thereby refusing Hegel and Blake. But that is inevitably a refusal of every truly modern thinker and visionary, and thereby a refusal of modernity, hence the comprehensive yearning of a contemporary Christianity for a post-modernity that is the ending of modernity itself.

The Universal Humanity

When Blake names Jesus as the "Universal Humanity" he is speaking of that incarnate Jesus who is both the source and the ground of a final actuality that Blake knows as "Experience," an experience that is not only the contrary of innocence, but which is the inevitable consequence of an absolute and total fall. The early Blake could know Jesus as the lamb of innocence, but as his vision unfolds this lamb becomes wholly the sacrificial lamb, and innocence itself becomes truly and finally an innocence lost, thus calling forth what he ever more fully knows as "Experience." Now experience is no longer the contrary of innocence, it is far rather its true opposite, and the Jesus who is the Jesus of experience is the Jesus who has descended into Hell. If this is the first full vision of the descent into Hell, it is also our first full vision of the totality of Hell, and now the incarnation of Jesus can only actually be known as an incarnation into that Hell. Not only are the heavens darkened as a consequence of that incarnation, now they are only visible or knowable as shadows or echoes of Hell, a Hell that is finally experience itself. Yet this is the experience that is ever more fully and more finally reversed by the Lamb, and the daughters of humanity can greet this Lamb as the self-emptying of eternal death:

> "We now behold . . . .
> Where death Eternal is put off Eternally.
> Assume the dark Satanic body in the Virgin's womb.
> O Lamb Divine! It cannot thee anoy. O pitying one,
> Thy pity is from the foundation of the World, & thy Redemption
> Begun Already in Eternity. Come, then, O Lamb of God,
> Come. Lord Jesus, come quickly."
>
> (*The Four Zoas*, VIII, 239-45)

This eternal emptying of eternal death is the "Self Annihilation" of God, a self-annihilation only fully embodied in the Lamb Divine, and a self-annihilation that is the self-annihilation of Satan, which is first fully recorded in this revolutionary breakthrough of *Milton*:

> I in my Selfhood am that Satan: I am that Evil One!
> He is my Spectre! In my obedience to lose him from my Hells
> To claim the Hells, my Furnaces, I go to Eternal Death.
>
> (14:30-33)

Now it is finally revealed that the self-annihilation of God in Christ is the self-annihilation of Satan, the sacrifice of the fallen and empty body of the Godhead, the very Godhead that is the repressive ruler of a wholly fallen world, and that is the final sacrifice that is apocalypse itself. So it is that "Milton," or the atoning Christ, in entering Satan can declare:

> Satan! My Spectre! I know my power thee to annihilate
> And be a greater in thy place, & be thy Tabernacle
> A covering for thee to do thy will, till one greater comes
> And smites me as I smote thee & becoming my covering.
> Such are the laws of thy false Heavens! But Laws of Eternity
> Are not such: know thou: I come to Self Annihilation
> Such are the Laws of Eternity that each shall mutually
> Annihilate himself for others good, as I for thee.
>
> (38:29-36)

This may well be the most revolutionary vision that has ever appeared in the world, and it is inseparable from a revolutionary vision of a New Humanity, an apocalyptic humanity that is the apocalyptic Jesus:

> Mutual in one anothers love and wrath all renewing
> We live as One Man; for contracting our infinite senses
> We behold multitude; or expanding; we behold as one,
> As One Man all the Universal Family; and that One Man
> We call Jesus the Christ: and he is in us, and we in him,
> Live in perfect harmony in Eden the land of life,
> Giving, receiving, and forgiving each others trespasses.
> He is the Good Shepherd, he is the Lord and master:
> He is the Shepherd of Albion, he is all in all . . .
>
> (*Jerusalem*, 38, 16-24)

Thus the Universal Humanity is One Man, whom the Christian calls Jesus the Christ, and that One Man is the consequence of the self-annihilation of Satan, or the self-annihilation of God Himself. Not only is this a *coincidentia oppositorum* of Christ and Satan, but also an unveiling of an absolute redemption or an absolute apocalypse finally reconciling and uniting all opposites whatsoever, as for the first time we are given a full and total apocalyptic vision. Even the Book of Revelation pales in the perspective of Blake's apocalyptic vision, and if Blake is the greatest interpreter of the Book of Revelation, this is unknown to New Testament scholars, to say nothing of theologians. The truth is that neither theology nor New Testament scholarship has even attempted to draw forth a genuinely apocalyptic theology, so here one must proceed without any professional guidance at all, which is perhaps true of every radical venture. However, we can learn from both Blake and Hegel that a genuinely apocalyptic theology will be vastly distant from all established theology, and that it will even effect an inversion or reversal of that theology, and above all so a reversal of everything that we have been given as God. The mere fact that both our theology and our Biblical scholarship are closed to this reversal is a genuine sign of the profound resistance to apocalypticism in our world, perhaps because our deepest modern apocalyptic visionaries are atheistic visionaries, yet this is nevertheless an apocalyptic "atheism," and one only possible by way of the birth of an absolutely new world.

Here, a new humanity will be vastly distant from an old humanity, as can clearly be seen in its very universality, and this is no abstract humanity, for all given or manifest abstraction wholly perishes in both Blake and Hegel, and with that perishing occurs an ending of every given or manifest humanity. While such a humanity may well be the object of our anthropological, sociological, and historical investigations, it nevertheless can be known in apocalyptic vision as finally being an illusion, and an illusion ultimately veiling an absolute apocalyptic transformation that is now occurring. For an old humanity has ultimately come to an end, an ending that we realize in becoming open to a new universal humanity, a humanity that is not only an apocalyptic humanity, but a humanity enacting an absolute self-emptying. Only this self-emptying realizes a truly universal humanity, and now an actual humanity is wholly silent and invisible apart from this self-emptying, or apart from what Blake names as Jesus the Christ. No doubt Blake would know our social scientists as undertakers, as guardians in the realm of the dead, yet their work is extraordinarily important if only in calling forth a universal death, one that is surely now undeniable, or undeniable to those who are awake. Not even Hegel could know that death, or know the actuality of that death, and it is just at this point that Hegel is now anachronistic, being wholly left behind by the advent of a world of universal death. Blake is the first visionary to call forth that world, or the first modern visionary to do so, but here universal death is inseparable from universal life, just as the ending of an old humanity is inseparable from the advent of a new humanity.

There is only one philosopher of universal death, and that, of course, is Nietzsche, but Nietzsche and Blake can be understood as polar twins, and most clearly so in their very apocalyptic vision. Nietzsche is our most purely apocalyptic philosopher, just as Blake is our most purely apocalyptic poet, each enacted a total and comprehensive fall as have no other visionaries, but that enactment in each is inseparable from the enactment of an absolutely new world, and if Blake names that new world as the New Jerusalem, Nietzsche names it as Eternal Recurrence. But Nietzsche's Eternal Recurrence is the very opposite of the archaic movement of eternal return, and is so because it is the consequence of the death of God, a death of God finally ending that transcendence that is the ground and goal of eternal return, and that transcendence is now totally reversed into the pure immanence of Eternal Recurrence. No one has ever understood fall more deeply than does Nietzsche, who can know the actual advent of humanity as a consequence of fall, one occurring with the very birth of our interiority or selfhood, an interiority that is the consequence of an original repression, when our original energy and life was blocked by the beginning of the social contract, hence that energy is internalized, and an original freedom is repressed and incarcerated within, and finally able to discharge its energy only against itself (*Genealogy of Morals*, second essay).

It is remarkable how coincident this understanding is with Blake's, but so, too, do Nietzsche and Blake share a vision of an apocalyptic body, a body that is a total and all comprehending body, one that is the very reversal of a primordial or original body and is so if only because it is not only the consequence of the whole movement of our history, but also and even thereby is the consequence of the death of God. Blake and Nietzsche alike continually enact an absolute Yes-saying to that body, and this is inseparable from an absolute No-saying to the inverted and empty body of an old humanity, an old body of eternal death only truly symbolized by the uniquely Christian God, yet a body that has become the prison of all humanity, a liberation from which is only possible by the death of God. Certainly Nietzsche knows an ultimate incarnation, and an incarnation in an absolutely new body, a body that is an apocalyptic totality, and if that body can be known as Eternal Recurrence and the Will to Power at once, is that the very universal body that Blake names as Jesus the Christ? That could be true only if the Will to Power is an absolutely self-emptying power, and Eternal Recurrence an absolutely self-emptying recurrence, but if this is manifestly true of Blake's apocalyptic vision, is it also true of Nietzsche's apocalyptic vision, too?

In his autobiography, *Ecce Homo*, Nietzsche ecstatically affirms that *Thus Spoke Zarathustra* is the consequence of the most ultimate revelation that has ever occurred, and while this work clearly intends to be an absolute reversal of Christianity, it embodies a new and apocalyptic redemption, and a redemption that is finally a redemption from the uniquely Christian God. All too significantly this is our only major modern work that is written in the genre of the original gospels, and if the redeemer is now named as Zarathustra, it is the Persian Zarathustra whom Nietzsche knew as the very origin of our history, an origin that a new Zarathustra has come to reverse, and to reverse it by an ultimate enactment of the death of God. In the section entitled "On Redemption," in the second part, Zarathustra reveals that the presence of time in a past and external form is the deepest obstacle to the realization of life and joy:

> "To redeem those who lived in the past and to recreate all 'it was' into a 'thus I willed it' that alone should I call redemption. Will—that is the name of the liberator and joy-bringer; thus I taught you, my friends. But now learn this too: the will itself is a prisoner. Willing liberates; but what is it that puts even the liberator himself in fetters? 'It was'—that is the name of the will's gnashing of teeth and most secret melancholy. Powerless against what has been done, he is an angry spectator of all that is past. The will cannot will backwards; and that he cannot break time and time's covetousness, that is the will's loneliest melancholy."
>
> (Kaufmann translation)

A spirit of revenge is born of this melancholy, what Nietzsche calls the will's ill will against time and its "it was," an ultimate rebellion against the very actuality of time, issuing in the refusal of time itself, and a consequent orgy of self-hatred as a broken humanity seeks to dissolve itself by ceasing to will. Zarathustra, in announcing a new redemption, speaks to the very madness of the vengeful No-sayer:

"I led you away from these fables when I taught you, 'The will is a creator.' All 'it was' is a fragment, a riddle, a dreadful accident—until the creative will says to it, 'But thus I willed it.' Until the creative will says to it, 'But thus I will it; thus shall I will it.'" (Kaufmann translation)

Perhaps this is Nietzsche's most illuminating statement of the Will to Power, one clearly calling forth a decisive distinction between the creative will and the destructive or the resentful will, and it is only the creative will that is the Will to Power, and this is a will to power absolutely transforming both consciousness and history. Accordingly, it is the very opposite of everything that we commonly think of as the will to power, and, indeed, the absolute opposite of that absolute power whom we know as God, and just as only the death of God calls forth or makes manifest the Will to Power, it simultaneously calls forth the God whom we most deeply know as the deification of nothingness. Now this is the very God whom Blake finally knows as Satan, but this Satan is the consequence of the Incarnation, only the Incarnation empties the heavens of the transcendent God, an emptying issuing in an ultimate darkness of the heavens themselves. Only then is the Lord of Heaven knowable or namable as Satan, for only then is an absolutely transcendent power an absolutely empty power, a power that Nietzsche can know as a pure and actual nothingness, but a nothingness only actually enacted in the death of God.

Only that enactment releases or embodies Eternal Recurrence, a recurrence in which all the names of history once again recur, but now they recur not as an eternal return to a primordial totality, but far rather as a forward moving recurrence to an apocalyptic totality; thereby, a new humanity is truly born, a new humanity that is an absolutely new world. And only now does "subject" or selfhood or self-consciousness truly come to an end, an ending known to Blake and Nietzsche alike, but an ending inseparable from an ultimate and apocalyptic darkness, a darkness that is nothingness incarnate, and one realizing a new and truly universal nihilism. Nietzsche is our only philosopher of that nihilism, or the one who most decisively draws it forth, that very nihilism against which the mature Nietzsche struggled most profoundly, and if this is a nihilism that truly broke Nietzsche himself, this is the Nietzsche who can finally sign himself as Dionysus and the Crucified. Can that signature possibly be the signature of Jesus? Did Nietzsche finally know his own deepest center as the Crucified, and is that the consequence of his discovery of an absolutely new humanity, or an absolutely new world? No one so prophetically foresaw the horrors of the twentieth century as did Nietzsche, and if our world truly is a new world, it is so most clearly as an actual embodiment of nothingness, a nothingness that is an actual and alien nothingness, or that very nothingness that has most profoundly been drawn forth by a uniquely twentieth century imagination.

Yet Nietzsche finally knew an apocalyptic *coincidentia oppositorum* between an absolute Yes-saying and an absolute No-saying, one that in *Ecce Homo* he identifies with Zarathustra himself, but Zarathustra is not the name of Nietzsche, not the name of anyone whom we can know as Nietzsche, nor the name of anyone whom we can know at all. For everyone is now no one, every actual "I" has now disappeared or is silent, a new anonymity is now truly all in all, and this as the consequence of the birth of a truly new world. If that world is the new humanity, it is the embodiment of an eternal death, surely the death of an old humanity, but apocalyptically only such a death could make possible the absolutely new. Both Nietzsche and Blake could celebrate that *absolute novum* with a total Yes, but this is a Yes inseparable from an absolute No, an absolute No that is an absolute self-emptying. This is the apocalyptic Yes that Blake celebrates as the apocalyptic Jesus or the New Jerusalem, but is this the Yes that Nietzsche names as Dionysus and Zarathustra, and is Zarathustra Nietzsche's name of the apocalyptic Jesus? Certainly not if we know Jesus as he has ever been known before, but if that Jesus has truly disappeared, this could make possible an absolutely new Jesus, and an absolutely new Jesus who is the embodiment of a new humanity and a new world.

Chapter Three

God and History

Dialectic and Theology

Nothing is more characteristic of our time and world than is the very
elusiveness of any possible ultimate ground. Indeed, it is ultimate
ground as such that is disappearing in our consciousness and society,
and disappearing with a seeming finality. Nor is anything else so fully
manifest in a truly postmodern world, and while this very disappearance is calling forth renewed quests for an ultimate ground, these
quests themselves are inseparable from a deep and ultimate ending.
Above all it is "God" that is most unspeakable in our new world, as
manifest not only in our literary and conceptual language, but perhaps
most comprehensively in a new technological language, a technological
language now becoming all in all, and all in all in a truly new totality.
While theological language is being renewed in our new conservatism,
it is extraordinarily doubtful if it has actually been resurrected, for
never has theological language been so distant from actuality itself,
or so moribund in its own intrinsic expressions, or so anachronistic
even within its own horizons. Is there no possibility whatsoever of a
genuine renewal of theology, no possibility of a truly new theology to
meet our new world, or is theology by necessity only possible as an
ancient theology, and hence only possible in a truly ancient or archaic
world? If so, is this not to say that there is no possibility whatsoever
of theology for us?

What is most manifestly missing from contemporary theology
is any actual opening to the truly new, at most this occurs only rhe-
torically, and never so as to engage God with our new world. It is as

though "God" is now our most forbidden theological category, the one least evoked in contemporary theological discourse, and one virtually absent from our critical theological language, and now even absent from our Biblical scholarship and criticism. Only orthodox theological language would now appear to be actual and real, but it is not only vastly distant from everything that we can now critically understand as the Bible, but equally distant from truly contemporary language and discourse, or from a language that is actually real in our world. Certainly this is a truly new theological situation, as for the first time in Christian history theological language is wholly alienated from its own world, and most clearly alienated from our actual historical world. While this has been ever increasingly real throughout the history of modernity, it has only been in the twentieth century that theology itself acknowledged this crisis. This most openly occurred in that dialectical theology that arose after the First World War, one deeply inspired by Kierkegaard, and by that Kierkegaard who was the first fully theological and dialectical thinker in the modern world. Hence, this theology begins with a proclamation of the end of Christendom, an ending that is the consummation of a full objectification or secularization of the Christian world. But that very ending makes possible a truly new dialectical negation, a dialectical negation of an objectified or secularized Christianity that is at bottom a recovery or renewal of an authentically Christian faith.

Although this dialectical theology has ended, is its renewal possible today, or could a truly dialectical theology meet the theological crisis of our world? Remarkably enough, there are very few dialectical theologians today, and this despite the fact that the ending of Christendom is far deeper and more comprehensive today than it was a century ago, and also despite the fact that our new world would appear to be far more the opposite of faith than all previous worlds. All too significantly, Barth repudiated dialectical theology when he embarked upon a Church dogmatics, and it can be seen that an ecclesiastical theology cannot be a dialectical theology if only because it cannot negate the dogma of the Church, indeed, can engage in no dialectical negation at all, except for Barth's dialectical negation of the orthodox doctrine of predestination. So it is that only radical expressions of Christian theology have been genuinely dialectical, and if this begins with Paul, Paul is the father of Christian dialectical theology, most clearly so in his dialectical understanding of sin and grace, a dialectical grace that can only be realized in the depths of sin, and a dialectical sin calling forth the necessity of the depths of grace. This is the origin of the Christian doctrine of predestination, perhaps the most dialectical of all Christian doctrines, a predestination absolutely necessary to make possible the depths of grace, a depth of grace that occurs in the depths of sin, and if only thereby a predestination inseparable from an eternal death, so that here a predestination to eternal life is inseparable from a predestination to eternal death, or the eternity of Heaven is inseparable from the eternity of Hell. This is the most offensive of all Christian doctrines, but as both Luther and Kierkegaard taught us so deeply, genuine Christian faith is inseparable from the deepest and most ultimate offense.

Not until the nineteenth century are we given a full and comprehensive dialectical theology, and if this occurs in Hegel and Kierkegaard, here there occurs a genuine dialectical negation of God; not only a negation of the God of Christendom, but also a negation of every God who is known or manifest apart from an ultimate negation, an ultimate and absolute negation apart from which there can be no authentic realization of God. Kierkegaard is that thinker who realizes the most ultimate internal or interior negation, a negation alone making possible a genuine faith in God, but this is a negation of every God who is manifest or real apart from the depths of this negation, one that for Kierkegaard inevitably entails a negation of every philosophical understanding of God, and above all a negation of the most purely philosophical understanding of God, which he knew as occurring in Hegel. The theological fate of Kierkegaard is truly fascinating, for if he can be known as the greatest purely religious thinker of modernity, he thereby was resurrected by early twentieth century theology, only to be marginalized by late twentieth century theology, not only because this is ever increasingly a Church theology, but also because it is a theology dissolving all possible dialectical thinking, and doing so if only because it is wholly incapable of actually confronting its own world. Genuine dialectical theology truly confronts its own world, as witness Augustine and Luther, but their dialectical theologies were conjoined with Church theologies, and hence were muted in their dialectical effect. Kierkegaard alone has given us a dialectical theology that is an anti-ecclesiastical theology, a theological thinking only possible by way of a radically individual movement, a truly individual and solitary movement ever more fully negating the Church, and one realizing what he could know as a pure interiority or "subjectivity."

Yet Kierkegaard's deepest conflict was an ultimate conflict with God, and with that absolutely transcendent God whom he knew so profoundly. At this point he is purely anti-Hegelian. Nevertheless, his is a dialectical struggle with God, one that he could know as a reenactment of Job, and just as Job is the only passionate No-sayer to God in the Bible, Kierkegaard is truly Jobean in his assault upon God. This is a dialectical assault inseparable from an absolute affirmation of God. Not until Kierkegaard is God fully manifest as a *horror religiosus*, a God not only inducing the most ultimate guilt and dread, but a God whose presence can only be known as an absolute assault, and an absolute assault upon our deepest interiority. While Kierkegaard is thereby in genuine continuity with Augustine and Luther, he nevertheless breaks away from every possible Augustinian tradition by knowing an absolute judgment that is wholly isolated from every possible grace, and at no other point did he more profoundly enact his own historical world. Here, Kierkegaard truly anticipated Dostoyevsky and a host of others who followed him, but we must recognize this as a genuine dialectical thinking of God, and thus it is inseparable from an ultimate and dialectical negation of God. But that negation as a dialectical negation is an ultimate affirmation of God, and this is a dialectical understanding of God that most deeply engages its own world. Just as Kierkegaard discovered an *Angst* that is a consequence of a naked encounter with a truly new and truly alien transcendence, an *Angst* that he could know as an encounter with the Nothing, that is an *Angst* that is universal in late modernity, or in the depths of that modernity.

These are the very depths that philosophically are most purely and most comprehensively enacted in Heidegger's *Being and Time*, perhaps the magnum opus of twentieth century philosophy, and one that was written during the period that gave us twentieth century dialectical theology. Heidegger was much under the impact of that theology, and even under the impact of the dialectical and apocalyptic Paul, as manifest in his 1920 lectures on the phenomenology of religion, and, here, Heidegger, unlike dialectical theology, could know orthodox Christianity as a reversal of an originally apocalyptic faith. So not only is Heidegger a descendent of Kierkegaard, but he is so most fully in his very understanding of *Dasein*, knowing that existence through "thrownness" (*Geworfenheit*) and fallenness and *Angst*, and even understanding authentic human existence as a "being-towards-death," which is clearly a uniquely Christian understanding, and an understanding that had an ultimate impact upon the twentieth century. While Heidegger is the only major twentieth century philosopher who underwent a full theological education, just as he is our only major twentieth century philosopher who is capable of a uniquely Christian theological thinking, so much so that he can affirm that the very idea of transcendence is rooted in Christian dogmatics (49), nothing is more absent from *Being and Time* than "God." For the first time in a truly major and comprehensive philosophical work there is a silence about God, and a new silence about God. Never before had there been such a deep thinking of Being accompanied by such a silence. This silence occurs throughout Heidegger's work, only being truly broken in his posthumously published *Beiträge*, which not only contains his most open attack upon Christianity, but which also has a concluding section on "The Last God." Yet Heidegger is nevertheless an apocalyptic thinker, not only knowing the end of metaphysics and even the end of philosophy itself, but also knowing a forgetfulness or oblivion of Being, and an oblivion ushering in an apocalyptic *Ereignis*, which in the conclusion of his work on Nietzsche he can identify as a "self-saving" of Being. That self-saving occurs in "the default" (*das Ausbleiben*) of Being, a default that is the destiny of Being, one finally realizing a "self-withdrawal" of Being, one occurring by way of an apocalyptic closure of the holy, but that very closure makes manifest the advent of the self-saving of Being wherein *das Sein gibt*.

Heidegger can even be identified as a radically Pauline thinker, certainly so in his understanding of guilt and fall, but also in his own genuinely apocalyptic thinking. Pauline language is that New Testament language that has most profoundly affected the modern world, and above all affected it as a dialectical language, a dialectical language in which an ultimate guilt is inseparable from an ultimate grace. But Pauline language is dialectical and apocalyptic at once, and it is precisely as such that it was resurrected by both Hegel and Marx, and if it is Marx who realizes the most naked and comprehensive of all dialectical negations, this can thereby be recognized as a Pauline negation, and most clearly so because of its deeply apocalyptic ground. Of course, dialectical thinking is banished from the contemporary world if only because of its association with Marxism, and if Marxism is our most revolutionary political thinking, it is also the most comprehensive dialectical thinking of the twentieth century, and that thinking offering the purest challenge to everything most deeply given in our world. Thereby it had a deep effect upon critical theology, even creating liberation theology, but the dissolution of Marxism is simultaneously the dissolution of liberation theology, and the apparent dissolution of every possible theological challenge to our world. Is this the consequence of the dissolution of dialectical theology? Is it just the dissolution of dialectical negation that has made impossible any genuine theological negation in our world? For a theology that cannot encounter its own world surely cannot challenge or negate it, and if for the first time in modernity the public identity of theology is wholly a conservative or reactionary one, is that, too, a consequence of the dissolution of dialectical theological thinking, or a dissolution of all possible dialectical negation?

It is important to understand that a dialectical negation is not a dualistic negation, or not a simple or literal negation, for it is an ultimate affirmation, but an affirmation only possible by way of the deepest negation, as here an absolute No and an absolute Yes fully coincide.

Hence a dialectical negation is a *coincidentia oppositorum*, a dialectical identity of an Absolute Yes and an absolute No, a dialectical Yes that is Yes only through that No, and a dialectical No that is No only through that Yes. We find such a *coincidentia oppositorum* in every genuinely dialectical way, and thereby we can understand that Christianity itself is at bottom a dialectical way. And just as Christianity has given us our most ecstatic visions of Heaven, so, too, it has given us our most horrifying visions of Hell, and if Christianity has initiated humanity into the most ultimate guilt, this very initiation is inseparable from an initiation into an ultimate and apocalyptic redemption. If Christianity has given us our most glorious vision of a cosmic Redeemer and Lord, it has no less given us our most horrifying vision of the crucified Servant and Victim, for the uniquely Christian Messiah is a truly dialectical Christ, a Christ who is at once the Christ of Glory and the Christ of Passion, and only dialectical theology has actually called forth such a Christ. So it is that both Luther and Barth could violently rebel against all scholastic or philosophical theology because it cannot know the Christ of Passion. Dialectical theology truly knows that Christ of Passion, as most fully manifest in both Kierkegaard and Hegel, but it is Hegel who most fully and totally knows God as the Crucified God, and precisely thereby Hegel who has given us our deepest dialectical theology.

While Hegel's dialectical theology, unlike Kierkegaaard's, can truly be known as an anti-theology, and most clearly an anti-theology as a theology of the death of God, it is just this ultimate negation of God that calls forth the most total and all-comprehensive Godhead in Western philosophical thinking, one going beyond even a Spinoza in its realization of the totality of the Godhead. Hegel's Absolute Spirit is quite simply the Godhead, but a Godhead actually realized only through the most absolute self-negation or self-emptying, a kenotic self-emptying known by the Christian as occurring in the Crucifixion, a knowledge that Hegel revolutionizes by realizing it as a universal absolute negativity. This is that pure negativity that is the source of an absolute self-negation or self-emptying, one apart from which God would not and could not truly be God, and one apart from which the world would finally be inactual and unreal. Hence this is a dialectical negativity releasing a dialectical negation that is the very opposite of a dualistic negation, a dialectical negation that it is true negates every God that is yet known to us, but it is precisely that dialectical negation that releases an apocalyptic totality of God, a totality that is first philosophically known by Hegel. True, Kierkegaard can know Hegel as the most purely and totally anti-Christian thinker, but Kierkegaard even as Marx absorbed a uniquely Hegelian thinking, a thinking apart from which neither Kierkegaard's nor Marx's would have been a genuine dialectical thinking.

Now it is true that Hegel can appear as a anachronistic thinker in the perspective of the cataclysms of the twentieth century, but there has nevertheless been a renaissance of Hegel in our world, not least so in our most deconstructive thinkers. If theological thinking is that thinking that now most resists Hegel, it is theological thinking that is most unengaged with our world. Ironically, it is philosophers such as Levinas and Derrida who are now our most open theological thinkers, and even as Heidegger is ever more fully becoming known as a theological thinker, it is only a strange and truly original theological thinking that can now be known as a genuine theological thinking. Even if it truly challenges all manifest theological thinking, it is precisely as such that it is a truly theological thinking. No such thinking has more potential now than a genuinely dialectical theological thinking, and as opposed to a phenomenological or a deconstructive philosophical thinking, it is dialectical theological thinking that establishes the most open horizon, one that can potentially be entered by all, as witness the horizons created by a Pauline dialectical language. Just as Pauline language is a consequence of an ancient prophetic language, a dialectical language conjoining an absolute No and an absolute Yes, it is the Hebrew prophets rather than a gnomic Heraclitus who are the deepest historical source of Western dialectical thinking, prophets who first truly negated every manifest or given God, a negation apart from which a uniquely Biblical faith would have perished.

It could be affirmed that it is only in dialectical thinking that an ancient prophetic language undergoes a philosophical rebirth or renewal. If nothing is more baffling about prophetic language than its full conjunction of an absolute negation and an absolute affirmation, a genuinely dialectical thinking profoundly illuminates that conjunction, and does so in its enactment of a *coincidentia oppositorum*. While such an enactment can be understood as being primal in Mahayana Buddhist thinking, it does not actually become realized in Western thinking until Hegel. Mahayana Buddhist philosophy created the most advanced logic in the world until the creation of the *Science of Logic*, and both of these are truly and purely dialectical logics, dialectical logics whose fundamental movement is negation, and an absolute negation that is finally an absolute affirmation. Yet Hegelian logic alone is a truly forward-moving logic, a forward movement embodying that *absolute novum* that was discovered by German Idealism. This is most deeply embodied in Hegelian thinking, a *novum* that was not even upon the horizon of a pre-Christian thinking, and did not actually enter Christian thinking as such until Aquinas' metaphysical discovery of the *novitas mundi*, but for Aquinas that *novum* is known only through revelation (*Summa Theologica* I, 46, 2), whereas for Hegel it is known through pure reason itself.

Christian Name of God

While Paul can justly be known as the creator of Christian theology, that theology almost immediately reversed itself, and reversed itself by transforming a forward moving apocalyptic movement into a backward moving primordial movement, as most decisively effected by its absorption of a Neoplatonic understanding of the Godhead. It would be difficult if not impossible to identify an ancient Christian thinker who was not a Neoplatonic thinker, or not a Neoplatonic thinker as a philosophical theologian. Hence the advent of Aristotelianism in medieval theology was a genuine revolution, one profoundly resisted by Neoplatonic theologians, and this is the perspective in which we can understand Aquinas as a revolutionary theologian, even if Aquinas was Aristotelian and Neoplatonic at once.

Certainly Neoplatonism is strongest in Eastern Orthodoxy, but this is the orthodoxy that almost wholly created Christian dogma, and this is a dogma that is truly Neoplatonic, and above all so in its understanding of Christ and the Trinity. Here, a Neoplatonic understanding of the Godhead is absolutely primal, a Godhead primarily known through the Father, that Father who is "unoriginate," the only person or mode of the Godhead that is from "no one," and precisely thereby the eternal generator of the Son and the Holy Spirit. Eternal generation is the deepest and most ultimate activity of this Godhead, an absolutely primordial eternal generation, therein Godhead itself is absolutely transcendent, and absolutely transcendent as an absolutely primordial Godhead, a Godhead that despite the movement of eternal generation is absolutely immutable, and hence one that cannot possibly be known through the passion and the death of the Crucifixion.

It would be difficult to imagine a theology more fully remote from the language of Paul, or for that matter from the language of the Bible as a whole, and yet there was virtually no awareness of this in the ancient Christian world, or none apart from its deepest heretics. It is also significant that Christian orthodoxy only fully or actually realized itself while Christianity was undergoing an ultimate transformation by becoming an imperial religion, and if now Church and State are truly united, this occurs in the first truly totalitarian *imperium*, for it is the first to realize an *imperium* that is internal and external at once. Christian orthodoxy was finally realized by that *imperium*, and just as it was Constantine the Great who introduced the orthodox formula of *homoousios* into the Nicene Council, it was the emperors who were the ultimate arbiters of Christian dogma, for Christian dogma became a fundamental instrument of imperial order. Thereby a Christendom was created in which political orthodoxy is inseparable from theological orthodoxy. If Heidegger can know "Latinization" as the passage of a uniquely Greek truth or *aletheia* into a Roman *imperium*, wherein the domination of command passes into the very essence of ecclesiastical dogma (*Parmenides* #3), this is not only the most dogmatic dogma in the world, but also the most commanding and purely authoritative dogma, and as such the expression of a truly new imperial and hierarchical Church. Christendom is the most intolerant and authoritarian of all pre-twentieth century historical worlds. Its very authority is inseparable from the authority of theological orthodoxy, and above all the absolute authority of an absolutely sovereign and absolute transcendent God. Now it is truly remarkable that not even Protestantism can escape this orthodoxy, or not an orthodox as opposed to a radical Protestantism. Just as the dogma of the Trinity is the very center of Christian orthodoxy, it is the dogma of the Trinity that is the most orthodox of all dogmas, just as it is that dogma that is most resistant to any possible interior, or imaginative, or conceptual appropriation.

Perhaps what is most revealing theologically about the orthodox Christian understanding of the Godhead is its very refusal of the possibility of the suffering or death of Godhead itself, hence it can know that passion and death as occurring only in the humanity and not the divinity of Christ, and this above all because of the absolute transcendence and absolute immutability of the Godhead. Here, a Neoplatonic horizon is fully manifest, one wholly alien to the pre-Christian world, including the world or worlds of the Bible, and yet no ancient theologian apart from Tertullian displays any real awareness of this problem. While the destruction of heretical theological texts may be one source of this lacuna, not even the deeply Biblical Augustine has any sense of the distance between a Christian Neoplatonism and the Bible, nor even any sense of the ultimate distance between the deepest poles of his own thinking, Paul and Plotinus. It would simply be inconceivable to the modern mind that it would be possible to integrate Plotinus and Paul, and yet Augustine realized a theological revolution by that very integration, one that is the deepest theological foundation of Western Christendom. Christian orthodoxy could only truly and finally end its Neoplatonic ground by ending philosophical theology itself, which is perhaps the supreme achievement of Karl Barth, and all too ironically, such an ending of philosophical theology was also embraced by Heidegger himself.

Of course, the dominance of NeoPlatonism in the West was first ended by Aquinas if not by Abelard, and nothing is more deeply negated by the birth of modern philosophy in nominalism than is Neoplatonism itself, a negation completed by the seventeenth century revolution in philosophy, so that Neoplatonism can return in later philosophy only in its most conservative and reactionary movements. Yet it does not truly perish in theological orthodoxy until Barth, and then most deeply perishes in Barth's Christomonism, one banishing every understanding of God that is not an understanding of Christ, and not an understanding of the Crucified Christ, thus making impossible any Neoplatonic understanding of the Godhead, an ultimate negation that has been the most powerful force in twentieth century theology as a whole. Many if not most theologians have known this negation as an ultimate liberation, but it only occurs after almost two thousand years of Christian history, and then occurs only after Christendom has finally come to an end. Already Kierkegaard could know that only the ending of Christendom can make possible a genuinely Christian faith, and at this crucial point Barth ever remained a Kierkegaardian, but both Barth and Kierkegaard are closed to the immense impact of Christendom upon Christian dogma itself. This is most concretely drawn forth by a Biblical scholarship demonstrating the chasm between the New Testament and orthodox Christian dogma, one overwhelmingly manifest in that dogma's ultimate transformation of New Testament eschatology, and inevitably Barth could not complete his dogmatics with its promised fifth volume on eschatology.

Indeed, there is at least one crucial point in which Barth and neo-orthodoxy remain within the horizon of ancient Christian Neo-platonism, and that is in understanding Godhead itself as an

absolutely primordial Godhead, a Godhead whose primordial movement is understood as the movement of eternal return, as manifest
in the movement of the Trinity itself. The very dogma of the Trinity
was created by Neoplatonic theologians, one that no expression of
Christian orthodoxy has ever challenged, and not even Barth himself
in his exposition of the Trinity in the first volume of his dogmatics,
although he does assault all philosophical understanding of the Trinity. But is the established dogma of the Trinity truly separable from
ancient Neoplatonic language and understanding? Above all, is it
not inseparable from a Neoplatonic understanding of an absolutely
primordial Godhead, one finally foreclosing every possible apocalyptic
ground, with the inevitable consequence that an apocalyptic theology
then becomes simply impossible? The greatest theological challenge
to the medieval Church was Joachism, one proclaiming the advent of
the final age of the Spirit, and just as this advent embodies the ending
of the age of the Son or the age of the Church, it inevitably challenges
the orthodox dogma of the Trinity, just as does every genuinely apocalyptic expression of Christianity.

This is most profoundly true of Hegelian thinking, yet Hegel is
the purest trinitarian thinker in the history of Christianity, and even if
this is a profoundly heterodox thinking, it is only Hegel who created
a whole system of thinking that is a trinitarian thinking, as not only
manifest in the fundamental Hegelian categories of Being-In-Itself, Be-
ing-For-Itself, and Being-In-and-For-Itself, and in a uniquely Hegelian
triadic logic, but equally so in Hegel's continual enactment of the three
ages of the Spirit, as for the first time apocalypticism is given a full and
total philosophical expression. Even in the *Science of Logic* the movement of Absolute Idea is a purely forward movement, one reversing
the backward or primordial movement of all scholastic thinking, and
one wherein primordial Godhead absolutely empties itself, and here
empties itself in the forward movement of pure thinking itself. Now
all Neoplatonic thinking is absolutely reversed, a reversal inevitably
transforming Christian dogma, as for the first time we are given a fully
philosophical understanding of that dogma, and even if this is a purely

heterodox understanding, it fully and comprehensively embodies the dogma of the Trinity as does no previous thinking. Yet Hegel's trinitarian understanding is inseparable from his purely conceptual embodiment of the death of God, a death of the Father releasing the totality of the crucifixion of the Son, and one wherein the Father passes wholly into the Son, but whose culmination is that resurrection that is the advent of the final age of the Spirit. Each of these movements is a fully and actually historical movement, nevertheless each occurs in a fully and purely conceptual movement, as for the first time ontology and history are wholly integrated and conjoined, and conjoined in the ultimate movement of a uniquely Christian Trinity.

Hegel can justly be said to have resurrected the doctrine of the Trinity, and it is noteworthy that his contemporary Schliermacher could relegate the doctrine of the Trinity to an insignificant appendix in his dogmatics, and thereafter the orthodox doctrine of the Trinity becomes virtually unthinkable as such, for Barth's exposition of the Trinity is his least original theological thinking, and only becomes alive when he is assaulting all philosophical understanding of the Trinity. Is it possible that the Trinity can only genuinely be understood through a purely dialectical thinking, and one inseparable from an ultimate negation of the orthodox doctrine of the Trinity, yet an ultimate negation that is a dialectical negation, and hence one renewing or resurrecting the Trinity in a wholly and even absolutely new identity? If it is the doctrine of the Trinity that most openly distinguishes Christianity, not only from Judaism and Islam, but also from Hinduism and Buddhism and a purely pagan Neo-Platonism, the doctrine of the Trinity thereby calls forth a uniquely Christian Godhead, a Godhead that is just as fully Christ and the Holy Spirit as it is the Father and Creator; but, whereas orthodox theology inevitably gives primacy to the Father, and primarily knows the Trinity through the Father, apocalyptic theology gives primacy to the Spirit, even if it primarily knows the Trinity through Christ. So it is that an apocalyptic and dialectical theology fundamentally knows the Trinity through the Crucified God, here overwhelmingly opposing all ancient theology, but the crucified God here finally realizes itself as a purely apocalyptic Spirit, or that Spirit that is an absolutely immanent Spirit, or that Spirit that is truly and finally all in all.

Orthodox trinitarian theology ever more fully draws forth a real distinction between what it knows as the immanent Trinity and the economic Trinity, an ever deeper distinction between that absolute Trinity that is within the Godhead alone and that Trinity that the Christian knows in revelation and redemption, one fully paralleling if not embodying the Neoplatonic distinction between Godhead and God. This is a distinction that Hegel ultimately ends, and he most deeply ends it by knowing the fullness of the Godhead in the Crucifixion, or the fullness of the Godhead as the Crucified God. While such an understanding can be understood as a Modalistic theology, a theology in which the persons or modes of the Trinity are known to succeed each other by fully passing into each other, it does make possible a full knowledge of the Father through the Son, the very goal of Barth's theology. But precisely thereby the Father ceases to be the Father and the Father or the Creator alone, or ceases to be the only person or mode of the Godhead that is "unoriginate," and therefore ceases to be known as the eternal generator of the Spirit and the Son, and if only thereby Father, Son, and Spirit are truly equal to each other, and truly interpenetrate each other. Yet this is possible only through the death or the transfiguration of the Father, the death of that Father who is the "unoriginate" or the "first," or the death of that Godhead that is and only is an absolutely sovereign and transcendent Godhead, and hence absolutely beyond any possible suffering or death. This is that death that realizes the true equality of the Son and the Spirit with the Father, one that the orthodox doctrine of the Trinity could never realize, but one that a dialectical understanding inevitably calls forth, and does so by its very negation of that Father who is Father alone, or its negation of the absolute sovereignty and absolute transcendence of the Godhead, a negation alone making possible a full understanding of the absolute equality and absolute interpenetration of the three persons or modes of the Godhead. This dialectical understanding is simultaneously an historical understanding, and is so by realizing a real and actual history of the modes of the Godhead, a truly transforming history, one in which each mode of the Godhead fully passes into the other modes, and it is this very movement that releases the most ultimate actuality, and does so by nothing less than an absolute transfiguration of Godhead itself.

It is fundamental to Hegel's dialectical understanding that it comprehend the profound transformations that have occurred in history, and one of these is the ultimate transformation of the uniquely Christian God, one fully manifest in the vast distance between an ancient Christian understanding of God and a modern understanding of God. And Hegel here understands a uniquely Christian history as evolving an ever more abstract understanding of God, this culminates in full modernity with the realization of what Hegel understands as abstract Spirit, and that he also understands as the "Bad Infinite," an infinity wholly alienated from finitude and the world, and one reflecting a truly self-alienated Spirit. But, it is precisely the self-alienation of Spirit that makes possible an historical self-negation or self-emptying of Spirit, one realizing a fully and finally historical embodiment of the death of God, which alone makes possible the full advent of Absolute Spirit. That advent is an apocalyptic advent, and one in which absolute transcendence passes into an absolutely new absolute immanence, but this is possible only by the absolute self-negation of absolute transcendence, and a self-negation that is a fully historical realization of the Crucifixion. This advent is the true Pentecost, and it is the consequence not only of the full historical evolution of Christianity, but of the evolution of the history of the world, a history that itself is the consequence of the absolute negativity of Spirit.

Hegel is that thinker who has most profoundly understood the ultimate transformation of Christianity, a transformation exhibited in no other historical tradition. This is a truly forward-moving transformation, one foreclosing all actual possibility of return, so that we can never return to a primitive, or an ancient, or a medieval Christianity, or even to a modern Christianity that is less than a purely and finally apocalyptic Christianity. But a purely apocalyptic Christianity is a truly universal Christianity, as most deeply understood by Hegel; everyone now embodies that Christianity, and does so by an inevitable enactment of the death of God, a death that could only be the death of the uniquely Christian God, a death finally actualizing a purely apocalyptic Spirit, one now realized in every deeper voyage of Spirit itself. Not until Hegel is a fully universal Christianity finally understood, but then it is only understood through a dialectical understanding of the self-negation or the self-emptying of Absolute Spirit, and one that Hegel maintains can fully be demonstrated both conceptually and historically. Such demonstrations are attempted in his university lectures, but they are most purely embodied in the *Phenomenology of Spirit* and the *Science of Logic*, works that have given us not only our purest dialectical thinking but our purest dialectical theology as well.

While we still lack a full or genuine understanding of that theology, and Hegel himself was unable to formulate it in a purely theological as opposed to a purely philosophical language, is this a dialectical theology that could be reborn in our world, and even reborn in the darkest abyss of our world? Or is theological thinking only possible today through a purely anachronistic movement, and therefore through a purely backward movement, one reversing everything that Hegel understood as the forward movement of Spirit, and one finally ending every possibility of an apocalyptic Christianity? Indeed, this would be a genuine consummation of orthodox Christianity, an orthodox Christianity coming into existence as an ultimate transformation of an original apocalyptic Christianity, and an orthodox Christianity ever more fully evolving a purely backward movement to primordial Godhead. Is it only in our world that such a Christianity can truly be all in all, and if postmodernity is far more purely and more comprehensively conservative than any expression of the modern world, does that make possible a truly new destiny of orthodox Christianity, and one echoing if not surpassing an ancient Christian Empire? Yet our orthodox Christianity is a truly new orthodox Christianity, one liberated from every interior, every imaginative, and every conceptual perspective, and one wholly at home with a totally technological world, a world ending every possible challenge, and ending every possible interior or exterior opposition. Now genuine heresy or heterodoxy is seemingly impossible, thus making possible a totality of orthodoxy never known before, and if this has ushered in an absolutely new anonymity, it is no less embodying an absolutely new emptiness, and an emptiness that is the very opposite of a kenotic emptiness, and is so in its all too literal actuality.

Hegel was the first philosopher to know the end of history, an ending even more deeply enacted by Nietzsche and Heidegger. Now, every truly forward movement is ended, or every forward movement that is an historical movement, and nowhere is this ending more fully manifest than in a postmodernity that can know itself as a liberated modernity, but a liberated modernity in which no ultimate forward movement is possible, or none that could go beyond a totally technological or a totally objectified world. Hegel could proclaim that art has come to an end, or the forward movement of art has ended, but this does not actually occur until the advent of postmodernity, an advent ushering in a desert of the imagination, and a desert of language, too, surely the most abstract and inhuman language that the world has ever known, a language consuming every possible remnant of interiority, or everything whatsoever that Kierkegaard knew as "subjectivity." Even Heidegger abandons the language of *Dasein* in his later work, and if Sartre renews it in *Being and Nothingness*, he abandons it in his later thinking, for with the full advent of postmodernity that subject that was the primal ground of a uniquely Western consciousness has truly come to an end. Is that an ending truly comparable with the ending of the ancient world, an ending most decisively effected by the advent of Christianity, and is the final ending of Christianity embodied in the advent of postmodernity, or is this an embodiment of an absolute darkness that Christianity first unveiled? Is the only truly religious or truly sacred epiphany that we can now know a pure and universal *horror religiosus*, and even if that horror is disguised with innumerable masks, is it not truly manifest in a new and comprehensive emptiness, and in a universal passivity, a passivity wholly disguised but nevertheless fully manifest in our world? Yet if this is an ultimate *horror religiosus*, it could only be an epiphany of what Christianity knows as Satan, and a uniquely Christian Satan who is an absolute nothingness, and a fully actual absolute nothingness.

God and Satan

While inquiring, in the *Genealogy of Morals*, into man's employment of God as an instrument of his own self-torture, Nietzsche remarks that man projected all of his denials of self and nature out of himself as God: "as transcendence, as eternity, as endless torture, as Hell, as the infinitude of guilt and punishment." These words repeat in their own distinctive way both Blake's prophetic attack upon the Christian God and Hegel's dialectical assault upon an alien and lifeless form of Spirit. Moreover, they illuminate a uniquely Christian epiphany of God, the God who in His transcendent majesty stands wholly over and against humanity, and before whom humanity is reduced to a abject condition of guilt and dread, and if that dread is an ultimate *Angst*, it is one that can be discovered only in a Christian world. Why is that historians of religion have failed to note that Rudolf Otto's idea of the numinous as *mysterium tremendum et fascinans* is drawn from the Christian vision of God and is paralleled nowhere else in the world's religions? Not even the Muslim or the Jew knows a deity whose very sacrality is absolutely opposed to the life and immediacy of our existence in the world. Nor does the Muslim or the Jew (with the exception of a Kafka), or any non-Christian, know that awesome and overwhelming guilt deriving from a naked encounter with an absolutely righteous Judge. Melville's enactment of Moby Dick, like Ivan Karamazov's rebellion against a truly cruel and destructive God, has inevitably cast a spell upon the modern Christian, because only the modern Christian has known a God who appears and is real only as *mysterium tremendum*, and a new *mysterium tremendum* occurring wholly independently of a *mysterium fascinans*, that awesome Lord whose absolutely sovereign power annuls and reverses the energy and life of humanity.

Thus Nietzsche can unveil Christianity as the absolute form of self-negation:

> The Christian conception of God—God as god of the sick, God as a spider, God as spirit—is one of the most corrupt conceptions of the divine ever attained on earth. It may even represent the low-water mark in the descending development of divine types. God degenerated into the contradiction of life, against nature, against the will to live! God—the formula for every slander against "this world," for every lie about the "beyond"! God!—the deification of nothingness, the will to nothingness pronounced holy! (*The Antichrist*, Section 18.)

Note that Nietzsche understands the Christian God as reflecting the lowest point in a descending series of divine epiphanies, one wholly other than an original Yahweh, whom Nietzsche could know as an expression of an early Israel's consciousness of power and joy and hope, but nonetheless continuous with the God of an apocalyptic Israel, a God whose final epiphany brings the world to an end.

Nevertheless, is it truly possible to speak of the Christian God, and the uniquely Christian God, as the deification of nothingness, the will to nothingness pronounced holy? Can we not apprehend a far holier will to nothingness in Buddhism? Yet the Buddhist is liberated from an abstract and empty nothingness, the nothingness of a wholly illusory center of consciousness or selfhood, by a realization of Nirvana or *Sunyata*, that all-encompassing, blissful, and total emptiness that is real precisely at the point where an empty nothingness is dissolved. Whereas, on the contrary, that Christian God whom Nietzsche knows, is only manifest and real by way of an absolute negation of the world itself, a negation inverting and reversing the life and joy of the body, reducing humanity to a purely negative and powerless *ressentiment*. Thus Nietzsche can know the Christian God as an absolute No-saying and an absolute No-saying alone, one absolutely opposed to every possible Yes-saying, or every possible life or affirmation. Clearly Nietzsche was obsessed by God, and by the uniquely Christian God, and if Nietzsche can be understood as a theologian, he is a purely negative theologian, and he has given us our most absolutely negative understanding of God. But Nietzsche understands our world with a depth and purity surpassed by no other thinker, and just as he is truly a prophet of the twentieth century, he has unveiled a late modern or postmodern epiphany of God that can be understood as the consummation of a uniquely Christian history, and one that in *The Antichrist* he understands as an absolute reversal of the original Jesus.

Nietzsche joins Kierkegaard in understanding the history of Christianity as a progressive inversion and reversal of Jesus, just as he also joins Kierkegaard in understanding a uniquely modern consciousness as a purely negative consciousness; indeed, both can understand a uniquely modern guilt and dread as the consequence of a uniquely Christian history, and one that is consummated in an ultimate crisis or an ultimate ending. Thus, each, at this crucial point, are truly apocalyptic thinkers, although Kierkegaard is a wholly negative apocalyptic thinker, whereas Nietzsche is a truly joyous one, and above all so in his proclamation of the death of God, that absolutely apocalyptic event that is a total transformation of history and the world. Nietzsche understands this apocalypse as the consummation of the totality of history, a history beginning with the advent of the "bad conscience" and *ressentiment*, and one ending with their absolute reversal, a reversal that he enacts as an absolute Yes-saying, and an absolute Yes-saying that is the apocalyptic joy of Eternal Recurrence. Nietzsche's proclamation of Eternal Recurrence is a pure reversal of the primordial movement of eternal return, and is so if only because it is only possible as a consequence of the death of God, a death of God finally ending the deepest source of *ressentiment*, an apocalyptic ending apart from which there is no possibility of an absolute Yes-saying.

Nietzsche's understanding of the relation between Yes-saying and No-saying is a truly dialectical one. Only the epiphany or the full manifestation of an absolute No makes possible the realization of an absolute Yes, a Yes that is truly Yes only as an absolute negation of that No, so that this No is essential to this Yes, a Yes that would be unreal and unrealized apart from an absolute negation of an absolute No. This is the absolute

No-saying that Nietzsche knows as the uniquely Christian God, one that is even renewed in Barth's understanding of the God of religion in his revolutionary commentary on Romans, a God of religion who is here clearly the God of Christendom, but one that is only fully manifest in late Christendom. And this is the very God whom Hegel could understand as abstract Spirit or the "Bad Infinite," but our most revolutionary understanding of this purely negative God occurs in the deepest apocalyptic vision of Blake, one that names the uniquely Christian God as Satan, and as that Satan who is the pure opposite of Christ. Remarkably enough, this occurs only after Blake had undergone an ultimate conversion to Christ, one delivering him from that Spectre whom he knew as the Christian God, and one making possible his deepest imaginative breakthroughs; but the most original one of these is his unveiling of God as Satan, an unveiling that is an ultimate ground of his final epics, *Milton* and *Jerusalem*.

Blake was the first prophet to envision the death of God, which occurs in his earliest epic, *America* (1793), and this is not only an apocalyptic but a truly joyous event, and a joyous event only possible by what he later envisioned as the "Self-Annihilation of God." That is the Self-Annihilation occurring in the Incarnation and the Crucifixion, and only as a consequence of that self-annihilation are the heavens darkened and emptied of all life and light, an emptying calling forth a full and final epiphany of Satan. It is seldom noticed that Satan is not actually or fully named as Satan until Jesus, a Jesus who was the first prophet to engage in an ultimate conflict with Satan, and the New Testament is alone among the world's scriptures in the primacy with which it calls forth Satan. But Satan only gradually enters the Christian imagination, only partially and fragmentarily being envisioned in the conclusion of the *Inferno*, and not fully envisioned until *Paradise Lost*, that very epic that most profoundly influenced Blake, and it is Blake's dialectical reversal of Milton's vision that calls forth his fullest and final apocalyptic vision. Already in *Paradise Lost*, God is envisioned as an absolutely solitary God; here, the Father is truly distant from the Son, that Son who in being generated by the

Father is here truly other than the Father, and it is only the Son who embodies an ultimate love and compassion, realized only through the suffering and death of the crucifixion. In *Paradise Lost*, Satan and the Son of God are truly polar opposites. Not only is each the very opposite of the other, but each is necessary and essential to the other, or each is essential to the ultimate acts of the other, as first occurring in a primordial war in heaven, and as finally occurring in an ultimate apocalyptic war. Indeed, it is not until Milton that we are given a full theology of Satan. This is the theology that Blake most deeply reverses, and reverses it by finally knowing Satan as Milton's Creator and Judge.

At no point is the modern imagination more unique than in the ultimacy with which it calls forth an absolute abyss, an absolute abyss that has been envisioned as an absolute nothingness, but an absolutely abysmal or absolutely negative nothingness, one infinitely distant from every scholastic understanding of evil as the privation of the good, and equally distant from every ancient vision of evil. Milton and Blake are those seers who most deeply inaugurate this vision, and they do so as genuinely Christian visionaries, for Christianity is unique among the world religions in the ultimacy with which it calls forth damnation, Hell, and Satan. While ancient Gnosticism could know the Creator as Satan, this occurs in a Christian Gnosticism, or in that Valentinian Gnosticism deeply inspired by Paul, and even if this is a profound transformation of Paul, no less a transformation occurs in a uniquely modern vision of Satan, but as opposed to Paul and the New Testament itself, now there occurs for the first time a vision of the totality of Satan. That totality is thereby an absolutely negative and all-encompassing abyss, and one that Nietzsche could know as being released by the death of God, when we are hurled into an "infinite nothing" and an empty space, and one in which night and more night is coming on all the while. Yet this is the very midnight that Nietzsche's Zarathustra can greet with an ecstatic joy, one that Blake himself had proclaimed well before Nietzsche, and it is Nietzsche and Blake alone among our visionaries who are most purely prophets of joy.

Blake and Nietzsche, in their own distinctive if not opposing ways, could know the Christian God as Satan, and this very knowledge is an ultimately liberating knowledge, one liberating us from the depths of an impotent passivity, and freeing us from an ultimate repression that Blake and Nietzsche each discovered. Yet that discovery occurs only with the realization of the death of God; it is only that death that opens us to the depths of our repression, a death apart from which we can never know the iron cage in which we are imprisoned, for apart from that death we can only know our own fetters as a transcendent and eternal power, as chains inseparable from existence itself. Both Nietzsche and Blake understood that the one primal act of Jesus is the forgiveness of sin, but this is his most offensive act, and the one most deeply reversed by Christianity itself, which initiated the world into an ultimate and absolute guilt. Blake could know that guilt as a reversal of both the Incarnation and the Crucifixion, and hence as a resurrection of Satan, and that is the very Satan whom Nietzsche knows as absolute No-saying, and a No-saying whose historical advent is the advent of Christianity. While it is the ancient prophets who created the "slave revolt" of morality, a revolt that is an absolute reversal of high and low, that morality does not become historically incarnate until Christianity, an advent that Nietzsche could know as the greatest of all historical catastrophes, and a catastrophe only reversed by an actual and an historical realization of the death of God.

Blake and Nietzsche, above all others, even including Kierkegaard, profoundly know historical Christianity as an absolute reversal of Jesus. Each could know the uniquely Christian God as the pure opposite of that ultimate life which Jesus enacted, as most clearly manifest in the absolute transcendence of that God, a transcendence reversing the primal words and praxis of Jesus. Thus the Yes-saying of Jesus becomes an absolute No-saying in Christianity, the forgiveness which he embodied is reversed into an absolute guilt, and the joy which he enacted is transformed into an ultimate impotence.

The very image of reversal can carry us into the center of a Christian transformation of Jesus. If we can now know that Jesus was an apocalyptic prophet proclaiming and enacting the dawning of the Kingdom of God, that is the very dawning that Christian orthodoxy transforms into absolute transcendence, then the forward movement of that dawning is transformed into a backward movement to a purely primordial transcendence. Clearly, this is a reversal of an apocalyptic movement into a primordial movement. Thereby we can understand that an apocalyptic Godhead is being transformed into a primordial Godhead, and this is an ultimate transformation of that Kingdom of God that Jesus enacted. Just as primordial and apocalyptic movements are truly the opposite of each other, the Godheads of these movements are opposite Godheads, and each can be known as the absolute "other" of the other. Thereby we can understand that Blake's Satan evokes an absolutely primordial Godhead, but a uniquely Christian primordial Godhead, for it is only this primordial Godhead that is the consequence of a pure reversal of apocalyptic Godhead, and hence here the primordial as such realizes a wholly new meaning and identity, one truly absent from every non-Christian apprehension of primordial Godhead.

A simple schema is illuminating here, and that is the apocalyptic movement from alpha to omega, but when that movement is reversed, alpha assumes a wholly new identity, and it does so because then alpha is a consequence of the reversal of omega, hence a truly new alpha. So it is that the primordial Godhead of Christianity is a truly new Godhead, one without parallel in either East or West, as most clearly manifest in the Christian doctrine of the Trinity. Here the Father is the only person or mode of the Godhead that is "unoriginate," and this ultimate difference of the Father from the Spirit and the Son gives the Father a pure transcendence unknown in either Yahweh or Allah, and equally unknown in either Brahman-Atman or *Sunyata*. Only the first person or mode of the Christian Godhead is truly *first* or truly absolutely primordial, hence the Father is the eternal generator of the Son and the Spirit. No such priority is possible in Judaism and Islam, or in Hinduism and Buddhism, because what the Christian knows as the Trinity is impossible in these traditions. Now if the dogma of the Trinity is the most orthodox of all Christian dogmas, it just thereby unveils the uniquely Christian Godhead, a Godhead that is absolutely primordial, and one found in no other horizon. But the absolutely primordial is the pure opposite of the absolutely apocalyptic, so that not only is the orthodox doctrine of the Trinity truly non-apocalyptic, it is truly anti-apocalyptic, and only arose as a reversal of an ultimately apocalyptic movement.

Now, if it is the very dawning of the Kingdom of God that is the source of the joy or "good news" of Jesus' proclamation, the reversal of that forward movement is a reversal of the gospel of Jesus, a reversal giving us what Nietzsche could name as *dysangel,* and what Blake could know as a pure repression. But that *dysangel* and that repression are possible only by way of a reversal of Jesus, hence this is a guilt and impotence impossible apart from a Christian horizon. It is an impotence that is grounding us, and that has ultimately grounded us, in the absolutely primordial, in the absolutely *first* or an absolute alpha, and one that is the true opposite of an absolute omega. Hence this is our ultimate bondage, and a bondage to a uniquely Christian Creator, or a uniquely Christian Lord, which Blake can know as the true opposite of the absolutely self-emptying Christ, and Nietzsche can know as the true opposite of the apocalyptic joy of Eternal Recurrence. Not only are Nietzsche and Blake our purest modern apocalyptic visionaries, they have also given us our purest apocalyptic visions of the uniquely Christian God. And if these are our most purely negative visions of God, they are precisely thereby apocalyptic visions, apocalyptic visions reflecting an absolute new apocalypse, and an absolutely new apocalyptic Godhead that is the very opposite of everything that we have been given as God. Only in that perspective can the uniquely Christian God be known as an absolute No or as Satan, and it is precisely the death of that God that releases an absolutely new apocalypse, an apocalypse that Nietzsche named as Eternal Recurrence and Blake named as Jerusalem.

Chapter Four

The Self-Annihilation of God

The Death of God

What can it mean to speak of the death of God? Indeed, is it even possible for us to speak of the death of God, and how could this occur at a time when the very name of God appears to be unspeakable? First, we must recognize that the proclamation of the death of God is a Christian confession of faith, and of a uniquely Christian faith in the ultimacy of the Crucifixion. For to know the God who has truly and actually died is to know the God who died in Jesus Christ, an ultimate and absolute death that the Christian knows as the one source of redemption, a redemption that is finally apocalypse itself. This is that unique and absolute death that Blake imaginatively enacts as the "Self-Annihilation of God" and Hegel conceptually and dialectically enacts as the negation of negation, an absolute negation that is an absolute negativity, and an absolute negativity finally releasing the third and final age of the Spirit. Once this age is fully and actually at hand, the death of God is all in all, and if this releases for the first time a truly universal Christianity, it does so only insofar as Christianity undergoes an ultimate transformation. For if the death of God is a uniquely Christian symbol it is, nevertheless, universally embodied in the fullness of modernity, and if that modernity is inseparable from an ultimately Christian ground, it is possible only by way of an ultimate reversal of Christianity itself. That is a reversal that not only Blake and Hegel call forth, but one that is at least potentially manifest throughout a uniquely modern consciousness and society, and if that society and consciousness is truly the ending of Christendom, that is an ending that can be greeted as an apocalyptic beginning.

Nothing is more difficult to draw forth than the actual and contemporary meaning of the death of God. This is above all true in a new postmodernity, a postmodernity seemingly ending all evocation of God, and if at no point is it more distant from a Nietzsche or a Hegel, at no other point does all ultimate language so manifestly disappear. Is that very disappearance a consequence of the death of God? If so, does it genuinely embody the death of God, a death of God that is seemingly no longer namable as the death of God, but that is nevertheless manifest in a new and comprehensive unnamability, or an unnamability of ultimate ground. While this can be recognized as a new silence, is it a silence in continuity with a mystical silence, a mystical silence reflecting a mystical abyss, but nonetheless a mystical abyss that is an absolutely transfiguring abyss? Never has a genuinely mystical abyss been so comprehensively embodied as is our abyss, and if ours is an abyss ending every distinction between depth and surface, or between height and depth, if only thereby it is a truly universal abyss, and so universal that it is apparently no longer namable as abyss itself. Not only is God no longer truly namable, but, so, too, an ultimate death is unnamable, an unnamability calling forth a purely empty death, an empty death reflecting a new and comprehensive anonymity. Or is it possible that this new death, too, is a consequence of the death of God, and even of that death of God that is a uniquely Christian death of God?

Christianity knows an ultimate and even a divine death as occurring in the Crucifixion. If that death can be understood as being continually renewed in a uniquely Christian history, and as finally becoming ever more comprehensive throughout that history, then a uniquely modern realization of the death of God can be understood as being in genuine and essential continuity with the Crucifixion itself. Now even if that continuity is possible only by way of a reversal of historical Christianity, such a reversal can be apprehended as being essential to Christianity itself, or essential to the universalization of Christianity, a universalization that is primal in both Paul and the Fourth Gospel. And if the Fourth Gospel and the genuine epistles of Paul are unique in the New Testament in so fully integrating crucifixion and resurrection, this is a resurrection inseparable from crucifixion, and a resurrection that both Paul and the Fourth Gospel know as becoming universal in the full and actual advent of Spirit. If this is the Spirit that Hegel knows as Absolute Spirit and Blake knows as the New Jerusalem, it is a Spirit only possible by way of an absolute negation or self-emptying, and one that is a self-annihilation of everything that is not fully actual in this Spirit. But that self-annihilation truly and finally ends everything that is not apocalyptic Spirit, hence realizing a new and total apocalyptic darkness, a darkness finally ending everything that is namable in an old world or an old totality.

That ending is all too clear in the New Testament, but is this an ending that can illuminate our contemporary condition, and our uniquely contemporary condition, a condition in which namelessness is seemingly all in all? Now if this namelessness is an expression of our nihilism, a new and comprehensive nihilism that is unique in history, such a nihilism can surely be understood as a new darkness, but can it be understood as a new apocalyptic darkness? For if it is a genuinely apocalyptic darkness it is inseparable from an apocalyptic light, just as the Buddhist can know Nirvana only by unveiling the depths of *Samsara*, an apocalyptic light can be realized only in the depths of an apocalyptic darkness, and it is that very light that calls forth and makes namable that darkness. In this perspective, no genuine naming of darkness is possible apart from an ultimate light, so that if we can truly name our darkness we can do so only by being open to that light, which is surely a fundamental reason why Nietzsche is such a primal thinker in our world, or why our most venerated writers are precisely those writers who have most fully or most purely explored our deepest darkness. At no other point is a dialectical exploration more fully manifest as an apocalyptic exploration, or an apocalyptic movement more openly manifest as a dialectical movement, and if full modernity has given us a genuinely apocalyptic way that is a truly dialectical way, that way itself can be a path into a new postmodernity, and can be so at just those points where postmodernity is most anonymous or most dark.

Already in Blake, God is finally unnamable, and unnamable precisely because of what Blake envisioned as the "Self-Annihilation of God," a self-annihilation not only reversing the Godhead, thereby transforming Satan into Jerusalem or the apocalyptic Christ, but ending everything that we have known and named as God. While that ending can be known as the redemption of God, or the self-saving of God, it is nevertheless a redemption that is the death of God, and thus God as God is now unnamable, or only namable in our most regressive moments or movements. Blake's "atheism" is a truly and fully polemical atheism, one assaulting everything whatsoever that in any way can be associated with "God," even discovering thereby a truly Satanic ground in every dimension of our life and world, for it is only the "Self-Annihilation of God" that calls forth the totality of Satan, only that self-annihilation reveals the totality of our darkness. So, too, it is only Jesus who truly reveals Satan in the ancient world, and if Blake finally came to know Jesus as that totally redemptive Christ who *is* Satan, that redemption occurs only in that crucifixion that is the self-annihilation of God. This is most fully manifest on the penultimate plate of *Jerusalem*, one whose ecstatic illumination portrays a *coincidentia oppositorum* of Christ and Satan or the Almighty and Jerusalem, a *coincidentia* that is apocalypse itself. Yet it is an apocalypse occurring only in the heart of darkness, and if that pure darkness is here finally manifest as an ecstatic light, it is so only through that darkness itself.

Blake's apocalyptic vision is inseparable from the totality of fall, a fall that is finally the fall of Godhead itself, so that a uniquely Biblical Creator is a wholly fallen Creator, as luminously revealed in Blake's illustrations to the Book of Job, so that on its eleventh plate the very glory of the Creator is most clearly revealed through his cloven hoof, as the most radical book in the Bible is for the first time called forth as a testament to Satan. Nor can Blake's apocalyptic vision truly be understood as a Gnostic vision, for even if it was Gnosticism that first identified the Creator as Satan, the Gnostic vision of Satan is a purely dualistic one, whereas Blake knows that dialectical Satan who is finally the Redeemer, and finally the Redeemer though his apocalyptic and dialectical union with his very opposite. All of us have become one with great Satan, enslaved to a cosmic but fallen "Selfhood," murdering the "Divine Humanity," until by "Self Annihilation" we come into Jerusalem. But it is the Creator or the "Lord Jehovah" who has bound the stars into a merciful order, bending the laws of cruelty to peace (*Jerusalem* 49:55), as Blake finally transforms a wholly fearsome Creator or Urizen into a merciful Jehovah, and Jehovah's salvation is the continual forgiveness of sins in the perpetual mutual sacrifice occurring in Great Eternity (*Jerusalem* 61:22). That perpetual sacrifice is the self-saving of God, a sacrifice that is the self-annihilation of God, and as such it is the most ultimate of all acts, and yet an act that is repeated or renewed in every genuine self-sacrifice.

Godhead only becomes, or is only truly actualized as universal Godhead through this sacrifice, a sacrifice that most deeply *is* the Godhead; hence, finally, Godhead is unnamable and unknowable as anything else, and in the wake of the historical or universal realization of this sacrifice, God is ultimately unknowable as God, and not simply ultimately unknowable, but ultimately unknowable *as* God. That is the knowledge that perishes in this realization, but so, too, perishes every full or fully actual consciousness of God, and every genuine naming of God, and every possible image of God. A critical history of modern philosophy knows this history as a progressive realization of the absence or dissolution of God, finally making an actual thinking of God impossible, or impossible in our purest or most genuine philosophical thinking. But this dissolution of God is certainly not confined to philosophical thinking, it occurs and ever more fully occurs in every realm of our world, and nothing is more historically unique in the modern world than its progressive and ever more total secularization, a secularization that is finally a dissolution of "God." Thus modern theology ever more fully comes to know history itself as an ultimate process of secularization, a history that Augustine could know as the City of Man, but now one manifest in a truly new historical consciousness, an historical consciousness apprehending historical events apart from any transcendent ground whatsoever, thereby apprehending a truly autonomous history, and thereby a history wholly independent of any ground beyond itself.

Theologically, the modern historical consciousness is most profoundly threatening in Biblical scholarship and criticism. Nothing else has so forcefully and so definitively challenged theological orthodoxy, a challenge already beginning with Spinoza, one that is comprehensively enacted in nineteenth century Biblical scholarship, and one culminating in our time in the virtual disappearance of all theological understanding in our Biblical criticism and scholarship. Whereas a generation ago there were theological orthodoxies that were open to genuine Biblical scholarship, now all such openness has ended, and there appears to be no real distance at all between fundamentalism and every form of Christian orthodoxy. But the new dominance of fundamentalism can be understood as yet another consequence of the death of God, for only that death makes possible a fully modern or postmodern fundamentalism, a fundamentalism knowing all critical thinking as an atheistic thinking, or all critical thinking that is a uniquely modern or postmodern thinking. Is it possible not to be sympathetic with this judgment, possible not to recognize it as a responsible reaction to a truly atheistic world, possible not to know a uniquely modern humanity as a humanity that has enacted the death of God? Yes, Nietzsche's Madman declares that all of us are the murderers of God, and are so in our actual consciousness and life, for as Hegel was the first to know, the modern consciousness itself is a consequence of the death of God, and is so in its full advent or birth.

Surely a new postmodernity is not an annulment of that birth. It far rather can be understood as its fulfillment, and not a fulfillment ending that beginning, but one carrying that beginning to its own consummation in a comprehensive realization of the death of God, and one so comprehensive that the name of God itself becomes unspeakable. If we cannot imagine a Nietzsche in our new world, this is in large measure because Nietzsche could so forcefully pronounce the

name of God, and surely Hegel is most alien to us because of his language of the absolute, a philosophical thinking of an absolute totality
that is thereby the thinking of Godhead itself, so that if Hegel is our
most ultimately theological philosophical thinker, he is just thereby
most distant from our world. But if we can know our world as one
that Nietzsche genuinely foresaw, and one only possible as the consequence of the ending of every possible absolute thinking, is this not
a world that could only be real through the death of God? Yet now a
death of God so universal that it is no longer speakable as such, no
longer speakable if only because the very word 'God' is so alien to our
new world, now even blasphemy has disappeared, or disappeared as
any possible blasphemy against God. Yet the blasphemy of *Finnegans
Wake* continues to resonate with us, and does so even for those who
cannot read it, and if this is the purest blasphemy that has ever been
written, it is a blasphemy only possible as a wake for God.

Can our world itself be understood as a wake for God, and a
wake for God precisely in a new silence of God, a silence of God
only broken in our revolts against this new world, and then never so
as to speak the name of God with either spontaneity or grace. Is this
yet another sign of how deeply forbidden the name of God is for us?
Just as Beckett could insist that *Waiting For Godot* is not a waiting for
God, that is a waiting that is impossible for us, and most impossible
for those who most believe in God, or most forcefully speak the name
of God, a speaking that is itself a witness to the hollowness of that
speech. Such speech resonates with an actual emptiness, and an actual
emptiness that is the emptiness of death, yet a truly new death, one
only present within the horizon of our new world, a world in which the
speaking of the name of God is the speaking of death itself. Can such
speech be understood as yet another witness to the self-annihilation of
God, and yet another witness to the actuality of that death, one truly
postmodern in its inability fully or spontaneously to pronounce the
divine name, and equally postmodern in the very comprehensiveness
of that silence? Is this yet another epiphany of what Blake and Hegel
knew as the Crucified God, but now a God so crucified as to annul all

possibility of resurrection, or all possibility of apocalypse itself? Surely ours is a darkness harboring no possible dawn, or none that could appear as dawning in any previous horizon, or are we are being called to a death of God more ultimate than any we have yet known, and more universal than any previous enactment of the death of God?

The paradigm of a new silence perhaps most openly makes manifest our contemporary condition, a silence inseparable from the advent of a new and totally comprehensive mass media. Now literacy itself is ever more fully passing into a semi-literacy, poetry is vanishing from our academic curricula, our philosophy is only truly open to a uniquely contemporary world, genuine opposition is absent from our political world, and our churches only seem capable of sanctioning such a silence. At the very time when a Levinas can call forth the ultimacy of the human face, face as face is becoming faceless, just as voice as voice is becoming voiceless, and language itself threatens to pass into a totally objective or purely quantitative language, an ultimate transformation that Kierkegaard already foresaw, and that once but now no longer could theologically be drawn forth as the ultimate enemy of faith. Above all it is the silence of theology today that in this perspective is most appalling. It is as though theology has quite literally come to an end, certainly come to an end in our academic and publishing worlds, and seemingly ended even in our pastors and priests. Now theological language is a truly anachronistic language, and perhaps even thereby a pure witness to a new death of God, or a new universalization of the death of God, one so universal that the very name of God is now absent from our speech, or absent from that speech that actually embodies our world.

Atonement

Sacrifice is the most universal movement of religion throughout the world, and while it occurs in innumerable forms, and in very different expressions, it can be understood as being our most ultimate religious ground, and as that ground embodying the most ultimate call to us. Certainly sacrifice is the deepest center of Christianity, which is why the primary symbol of Christianity is the cross, and the cross is at once a universal and a unique symbol, universal in evoking an absolute sacrifice, but unique in knowing this sacrifice as occurring in incarnate Godhead, and occurring as the deepest and most ultimate act of that incarnate Godhead. Hence, the Christian symbol of the cross is inseparable from a uniquely Christian incarnation, an incarnation culminating in crucifixion, or culminating in that resurrection that is the apocalyptic realization of crucifixion. Yet at no other point has the great body of Christianity so reversed its original ground, knowing incarnation and crucifixion as culminating in ascension, and an ascension to an absolutely primordial heaven, an eternal life that is the very opposite of the eternal death of the crucifixion, and an absolute transcendence that is the very opposite of both an apocalyptic immanence and a truly incarnate body or flesh. Only Christianity embodies such an absolute reversal of its original ground, and if orthodox Christianity has never been able either to envision or to know a truly incarnate Godhead, this is the very Christianity that knows the absolute transcendence and the absolute immutability of God, an immutability foreclosing all possibility of either the incarnation or the crucifixion of Godhead itself.

Nothing is more revealing of this Christianity than its understanding of the atonement, an atonement occurring in the crucifixion, yes, but there occurring only as the sacrifice of the humanity and not the divinity of Christ. Here atonement is the annulment of the sin of humanity, and the annulment of that eternal death that is the consequence of original sin, an annulment returning humanity to its pre-sinful, or original, or primordial condition. Once again we can apprehend a new primordial movement reversing an original apocalyptic movement, but here a primordial movement dissolving every possible apocalyptic horizon, and one making impossible any possible apocalypse, an impossibility that is the inevitable consequence of understanding the atonement as a movement of eternal return. That very Kierkegaard who understood

Christendom as a truly pagan Christianity, understood paganism itself as a backward movement of recollection, as opposed to the forward movement of a uniquely Christian repetition, yet here repetition and recollection are the same movement, although in opposite directions, for what is recollected has been, and is repeated backwards, but true repetition is recollected forwards, and it is this repetition that is the core of every genuine Christian dogma.

No theologian has yet been able to incorporate this Kierkegaardian understanding into an understanding of Christian dogma, but have we yet been given a theological understanding of a uniquely Christian atonement, an atonement only possible by way of the uniquely Christian Christ, or the truly crucified Christ? It could be said that only Barth even attempts such a radical theological venture, and this he does in his truly new understanding of election or predestination, one wherein the very Godhead of Christ is eternally predestined or elected to an eternal damnation, an eternal damnation in which Christ himself is guilty of that contradiction against himself that is original sin, and a damnation suffered so as to make damnation impossible for all others (*Church Dogmatics*, II, 2). Barth can know this election as the very essence of the gospel, the very source of a uniquely Christian Yes, and it is so only by the full and actual damnation of the Son of God, that Crucified Christ whom Barth can know as the fullness of the Godhead. Certainly this is the most radical understanding of the atonement that Christian theology has yet given us, and this is a uniquely Christian understanding of sacrifice or atonement, and one understanding a uniquely Christian Godhead as eternally embodying an absolute sacrifice, and an absolute sacrifice of Godhead itself. Note that for Barth, as opposed to all previous theology, Christ becomes truly and ultimately guilty as the atoning Victim, and if Barth more fully than any other modern theologian understands the absolute No of God, that is a No enacted only to make this Yes possible, and therefore the first and last word is Yes and not No.

It cannot be denied that the Christian understanding of the atonement is the understanding of an annulment of an absolute sin, but is that annulment a dissolution or a transfiguration of sin, does it return us to our original and pre-fallen condition, or does it transform an old Adam into a truly new Adam, thus making possible the advent of an absolutely new world? Such a new world or new creation could only be the consequence of a transfiguration rather than a dissolution of sin, and a transfiguration not only effected by the incarnate and crucified Christ, but fully embodied in that Christ, a Christ whom Paul could apocalyptically know as the new Adam, and a new Adam absolutely transcending a pre-fallen or original Adam. Here, the category of the body is all important, is Christ's body a primordial or an apocalyptic body, or can it be both at once, and a primordial and an apocalyptic body as a truly total body? Now just as Christianity has profoundly resisted the Incarnation throughout its history, or resisted it as a full and final incarnation in the body or in "flesh," it has ever refused every possibility of apocalyptic body, and every possibility of a truly new as opposed to a primordial creation. We can discover this refusal in every orthodox theologian, including Barth, but is this refusal a refusal of every possible body, or every possible body other than the original or primordial body of Adam?

Gnosticism has given us our purest loathing of the body, but this Gnosticism is a uniquely Christian Gnosticism, and it surely has a genuine parallel in Christian Neoplatonism, even including Augustine himself. Could this be understood as a consequence of the reversal of the Incarnation, one possible for Christianity alone, and one real-izing not simply a sense of the pollution of the body, but far rather a sense of the body itself as an embodiment of sin, so that Augustine could understand orgasm itself as a consequence of the Fall. This is a Fall creating a dichotomy between the body and the soul, a violently discordant state in which passion and the mind are wholly unlike but wholly commingled, thereby making possible a new pleasure surpassing all physical delight, a pleasure culminating in a climax wherein the mind is overwhelmed (*City of God*, XIV, 16). This is the very moment and condition that makes possible the transmission of original sin, the one moment when the mind is wholly absent, and we are body alone, a body that is pure lust, and a body in which we are least free. Each of us has our origin in this moment of pure body or pure lust, thereby the original sin of Adam becomes the sin of all, and our bodily origin becomes the very opposite of our origin in God's creation. This Augustinian and deeply Neoplatonic understanding had an enormous impact upon subsequent Western history, and not only is body here known as a deeply guilty body, but a body wholly incapable of transfiguration, and thus the resurrected body could only be a purely non-sexual body, or a body that is pure spirit alone.

Again and again Blake enacts a uniquely Christian God whose epiphany is inseparable from a condemnation of the body, and above all a condemnation of sexual delight, and Blake understands this condemnation as a reversal of the Incarnation, one transforming body itself into sin and sin alone. No such condemnation of the body is manifest in either Judaism or Islam, or in the ancient world as a whole until the advent of Christianity, so that if it is the uniquely Christian God who induces an ultimate bodily guilt, a guilt far transcending every ancient or archaic sense of pollution, this is a guilt finally inseparable from a uniquely Christian atonement. Does that atonement liberate us from our body, and from that body that is a body of sin, a bodily or sexual sin that is the purest source of our enslavement — for it is libido, or a purely bodily energy, that is the immediate source of our impotence — and is that the libido that is annulled by a uniquely Christian atonement? Blake could know that atonement, or that atonement in its orthodox Christian form, as a transformation of a truly bodily energy into a sinful and guilty passion, one liberating us by dissolving or reversing bodily energy, so that our bodies then become truly inverted, and such an orthodox body of Christ is truly a body of death. Yet Blake reversed this orthodox understanding of atonement, and most deeply did so in his apocalyptic understanding of atonement, an atonement that is the atonement of Satan or the uniquely Christian Creator, one transfiguring rather than dissolving that ultimate body of eternal death, a transfiguration that is the resurrection of the body itself.

Not until the advent of modernity does an understanding arise of a deep conflict or opposition within the Godhead, or within the deepest depths of the Godhead, an opposition between the negative and the positive poles of the Godhead, and one wherein it is the negative pole of the Godhead that is the ultimate origin of evil. This understanding is first fully realized by Boehme, who had a deep impact upon both Schelling and Hegel, but it is Hegel who first comprehensively realizes this truly dialectical understanding of the Godhead, and one in which absolute affirmation and absolute negation fully pass into each other. Just as Hegel is the first philosopher to understand the death of God, he understands that death as the consequence of a divine and absolute No, but an absolute No finally realizing an absolute Yes, and an apocalyptic Yes that is the absolute transfiguration of everything whatsoever. Here, we can apprehend a uniquely Hegelian understanding of the atonement, one wherein only the death of God can make possible the ultimate transfiguration of the Godhead, so that this death is an absolutely atoning death, and one that is ultimately an atonement of Godhead itself. Now just as Hegel can know abstract Spirit or the "Bad Infinite" as the deepest ground of self-alienation and self-estrangement, it is precisely the reversal of that ground that effects atonement, but that is finally a reversal of the negative pole of the Godhead, a negative pole that only fully appears or is fully manifest with the advent of the age of the Spirit.

Thus, both Blake's "Satan" and Hegel's "Bad Infinite" are truly parallel with each other, and just as Hegel only enacts the "Bad Infinite" in the purely abstract thinking of the *Science of Logic*, Blake only fully enacts Satan on the most cryptic and baffling plates of *Milton* and *Jerusalem*. While this seemingly confines both Blake and Hegel to a an esoteric realm, it is nevertheless true that at no other point do they more fully engage both their world and ours. Indeed, if at only this point Hegel and Blake are truly our contemporaries, and most contemporary in their very understanding of atonement, a seemingly anachronistic dogma wholly removed from our world, and yet here a dogma deeply illuminating our world, and most illuminating it by envisioning an ultimate reconciliation or atonement only possible in the deepest depths of alienation and darkness.

No such understanding of atonement is possible apart from those depths, but a uniquely Christian understanding of atonement has never been possible apart from an understanding of the depths of sin. If it is Paul who first formulates a theological understanding of this atonement, it is Paul who has given us our purest understanding of sin, an ultimate and absolute sin that is inseparable from an ultimate and absolute grace. That is the dialectical conjunction, or dialectical *coincidentia oppositorum*, that a uniquely Christian atonement inevitably calls forth, one that is even present in Barth's *Church Dogmatics*, although not openly present in any other dogmatics of the Church. Barth is our only modern theologian of damnation, and if he most deeply understands damnation as the damnation of Christ, a damnation eternally predestined by Godhead itself, this is a damnation far more meaningful to a new postmodernity than to the great body of modernity, for it is postmodernity that most embodies a fully actual and truly universal emptiness, an abstract emptiness going beyond what was once manifest as a self-estrangement or self-alienation, and thus one at least potentially open to a uniquely Christian enactment of damnation. If a uniquely Christian atonement is inseparable from a uniquely Christian damnation, and if that atonement is ultimately inseparable from the atonement of Godhead itself, and an atonement of the negative depths of the Godhead, that is a self-saving of God only possible in the ultimate depths of a purely negative abyss. If it is only postmodernity that universally embodies such an abyss, is it only postmodernity that can finally know such a self-saving of God?

The very name of God is unknowable and unsayable in that abyss, for if that is an abyss in which Godhead itself is undergoing an ultimate transformation, then God can never therein appear or be real as God, and cannot do so if only because a truly transformed Godhead must be wholly other than every possible God, or wholly other than everything that has been named as God. If it is Godhead itself that is undergoing atonement in this ultimate transformation, an atonement that is an absolute sacrifice, that could occur only when Godhead is wholly other than itself, and wholly other than itself as a truly self-divided or self-alienated Godhead, an absolutely dichotomous Godhead that only as such could actually embody an absolute sacrifice. Hegel purely understands this dichotomy in his understanding of the self-negation of Spirit, a self-negation in which Spirit kenotically becomes its own other, therein Spirit exists "for-itself," but only insofar as it *is* its own opposite. Thus Spirit, which exists originally and eternally "in-itself," must and does become wholly other than itself, yet just as it remains identical with itself in its own absolute otherness, it is this opposition within itself that is the source of its movement and life, and if this is an ultimate and absolute movement of self-negation or self-emptying, it is precisely as such that the forward and apocalyptic movement of Spirit occurs.

Is this not a fully conceptual understanding of what the Christian knows as atonement? Therein, of course, the atonement is a universal process of self-negation or self-emptying, and a self-emptying and self-negation that is an absolute sacrifice, an absolutely atoning sacrifice that Blake, too, envisions as a universal and wholly comprehensive movement. But nothing that we can know as "God" is manifest in this atonement, an atonement actually embodying the death of the transcendent God, a death that is the absolute self-negation or self-emptying of transcendent Godhead, apart from which no ultimate or absolute atonement is possible, and apart from which no absolute sacrifice is possible. Only this absolute sacrifice makes possible an absolute apocalypse, an apocalypse finally bringing to an end every Godhead that is not apocalyptic Godhead, and thus one ending every ground of primordial Godhead, thereby ending every memory or recollection of that Godhead. Has the time arrived at last when such a memory has wholly disappeared, or disappeared as a real and actual memory or recollection, and even disappeared with the very advent of our new world? Surely memory is extraordinarily shallow in this world, and it can be asked if a deep memory is now possible at all, and if such memory is now all too fragmentary and rare, can this be understood as an inevitable consequence of the final ending of primordial Godhead itself? Indeed, is it not an inevitable consequence of an absolute self-negation or self-emptying of the Godhead, and if that self-emptying can be understood as an absolute sacrifice, is not the absolute emptying of primordial ground an inevitable consequence of that sacrifice? Is this the sacrifice to which we are now being called, and one that is even reflected in our new world, but openly reflected only in a new and all comprehending passivity, a passivity that is the very opposite of an actual sacrifice, yet one perhaps making possible a new sacrifice, a sacrifice apart from which we are now without any hope whatsoever?

The Forgiveness of Sin

A full apocalypticism realizes an absolute polarity or an absolute opposition between new world and old world, or new æon and old æon, one that Paul can know as an opposition between "flesh" and Spirit, and one calling forth truly new realizations of both Spirit and "flesh." Only then is it possible to know an absolute guilt or an absolute darkness, but that very guilt is now known through the sacrifice of Christ, an atoning sacrifice first calling forth that absolute guilt that it assuages. Paul deeply grasps the relation between sin and grace as a purely dialectical relation, for this is an apocalyptic grace occurring at the very center of an apocalyptic darkness, and a darkness only revealed or made manifest in the Crucifixion, a crucifixion that Paul knows as an apocalyptic crucifixion, and as such the very inauguration of the new æon, but one nevertheless occurring in the deepest depths of an apocalyptic darkness. So it is that a uniquely Christian grace occurs only in the depths of sin, depths that are called forth by this grace, and therefore depths only truly manifest through this grace. Thus if an absolutely guilty consciousness is first recorded by Paul, this is a consequence of the absolute grace of the Crucifixion, a crucifixion apart from which we would be uninitiated into our own negative depths, or our own absolute darkness. Augustine was the first truly Pauline theologian, and nothing is more primal for Augustine than the absolute polarity or the absolute opposition between sin and grace, each is the true opposite of the other, and yet each is only truly realized through the other. Hence an overwhelming sense of sin is a consequence of grace, an absolutely free and an absolutely justifying grace, and only through that grace do we realize the depths and the ultimacy of that sin to which we are enslaved.

While it is Paul who created the Christian understanding of predestination, we are not given a theological doctrine of predestination until Augustine, one that had an enormous impact upon Western Christianity, and it is not until the seventeenth century that one can discover a Western Christian theologian who is not a theologian of predestination. This doctrine is inseparable from an acceptance of absolute sin, a sin so absolute that we cannot possibly escape or transcend it. That transcendence can be effected by the grace of God alone, hence it is wholly beyond our own power, and can be realized only by the eternal predestination of God, a predestination apart from which our only possible end or destiny is damnation itself. Here, it is fully manifest that a uniquely Christian redemption is inseparable from a uniquely Christian damnation, and it is God Himself who is the ultimate source of both damnation and redemption, a uniquely Christian God who cannot be the God of redemption apart from being the God of judgment and damnation. Even if Augustine did not explicitly formulate a doctrine of double predestination, a predestination to eternal life and to eternal death, double predestination is an inevitable consequence of this theological understanding, and is so because of the absolute sovereignty of God.

Augustine goes beyond his Neoplatonic predecessors in understanding Godhead itself as absolute act, an act that is the eternal act of God, and one comprehending all of the acts of God, including creation and redemption, but so, too, is thereby included the eternal judgment of God, and an eternal act of judgment inseparable from an eternal act of redemption. So it is that God in willing eternal redemption inevitably and necessarily wills eternal judgment, a judgment necessarily occurring in response to evil and sin, and while Augustine will not affirm that God wills evil, he again and again speaks of God's "permission of evil" (*The Enchiridion* XCVI), a permission apart from which there could be no evil. Damnation is the inevitable consequence of our rebellion against God, a damnation that is everyone's through original sin, and a damnation from which we can be freed only by the grace of God, a grace that is only possible through predestination, for apart from predestination the sinner would be wholly closed to grace, and necessarily so by virtue of the very nothingness of our fallen and rebellious will. As Augustine remarks in the *Predestination of the Saints* (XIX), the only difference between grace and predestination is that predestination is the preparation for grace, while grace is the gift itself. Predestination alone is the source of the conversion and transformation of the sinful will, the potentiality for which is in no way whatsoever present in the empty nothingness of the fallen will, and it is just because the knowledge of predestination teaches us that no one is saved except by undeserved mercy that we can realize the utter vacuity of sin. So it is that Augustine can close the *City of God* with the affirmation that the redeemed saints in the Heavenly City, while having no sensible recollection of past evils, will nevertheless know the eternal misery of the damned, for how else could they sing the mercies of the Lord?

Predestination may well be the most horrible of all dogmas, perhaps the purest *horror religiosus*, but every truly major Western Christian theologian is a theologian of predestination, and inevitably a theologian of predestination if only because of those ultimate depths of evil and nothingness that are seemingly only fully manifest in the West. And only by understanding those depths is it possible to understand a uniquely Christian forgiveness of sin, a theological understanding that Barth alone has given us in the twentieth century, but one apparently absent from every contemporary theological school or tradition, and perhaps most manifestly absent from contemporary Christian preaching. That preaching is historically unique if only because of the absence of all language about damnation and Hell, but is it possible for the Christian to know forgiveness apart from knowing damnation, or possible to know grace apart from the ultimate depths of sin? There is a deep paradox here, for just as a knowledge of grace is here inseparable from a knowledge of sin, the depths of grace occurs only in the depths of sin, and apart from those depths no such grace could occur at all. If it is Christianity that ends any possible innocence, this occurs at the very center of Christianity, for it occurs in an ultimate redemption from an ultimate damnation, and that very redemption reveals the universality of damnation, and a damnation that does not disappear from the Christian consciousness until the full secularization of Christianity.

Yet at the very time that this disappearance occurs, our deepest and purest imaginative enactments have been enactments of an ultimate emptiness or an ultimate chaos or an ultimate nothingness, enactments wherein a distinctively Christian damnation is renewed, but renewed wholly apart from every established Christian horizon of redemption. If only thereby, our given Christian language about redemption has become hollow and unreal, and if only recently it was possible to discover Christian poets, that is seemingly impossible today, and even if poetry is now alien to our world, it is precisely in poetry that our richest language occurs.

Could the dark language of full modernity, and the uniquely dark language of full modernity, be a reflection of a redemption occurring in the heart of darkness, a redemption inseparable from that darkness, and a redemption only possible in the depths of that darkness? Is this a redemption that can only be known theologically by knowing the absolute No of God, a No to which contemporary theology is wholly closed, a closure that is perhaps the closure of theology itself, but also a No that only a Heidegger and a Sartre have known among twentieth century philosophers, just as Sartre and Heidegger are our only contemporary philosophers who have known the interior depths of consciousness. Surely there is a genuine correlation between an absolute No and everything that we can know as interior depth, and it must never be forgotten that Augustine was the first philosopher of subject or self-consciousness, the first thinker to explore an interior consciousness, just as he was the creator of the genre of autobiography. Not until Augustine is redemption known as occurring in the depths of our interiority, depths that were closed to Augustine himself until he became overwhelmingly aware of those interior bonds that so enslaved him. It was that awareness that opened him to his own interior depths, an opening initiating the West itself into a truly new subject or a truly new self-consciousness. If that self-consciousness is ending in our own world, this is the consummation of a vast interior voyage, but as that voyage progressed a purely interior negativity or self-laceration became ever more real, one becoming all in all in late modernity, yet it is just such a negativity that the primal poets and artists of that modernity could so profoundly transfigure, a transfiguration issuing in a uniquely modern or late modern Yes.

Is every such Yes impossible today? Could a subterranean redemption be occurring, a redemption so buried that it is wholly silent and invisible, or only manifest in a surface closed to all depth, or a surface in which there is no distinction between surface and depth, a truly new surface, and a truly new empty and vacuous surface, one manifest throughout our new world, as we are quite literally becoming empty and hollow? Now the very word 'sin' is vacuous, and the word 'evil' virtually unpronounceable. Ethical thinking itself has become conceptually impossible, except for that Levinas who can recreate ethical thinking only by way of an absolute return to an absolutely primordial "Infinite," a return inseparable from an inversion of our world, but a return perhaps made possible by that very inversion. Is there any genuine poet or genuine thinker today who can actually affirm our world? If not, is this not a condition truly paralleling the condition of that world in which Christianity was born? Nietzsche could justly know the original Christian gospel as *dysangel*, but as such it was truly revealing of its own world. Perhaps there were no horrors in the ancient world truly comparable to the magnitude of the horrors of the Roman Empire, and surely never such dark thinking among the ancients until that time; even the epic celebration of *The Aeneid* is the celebration of an absolutely imperial power. If this was a world that gave birth to an absolutely other-worldly Gnosticism, and a truly other-worldly Neo- platonism, it was a world undergoing an ultimate crisis or ending. Augustine could know the Roman Empire as a consequence of God's providence so as to make possible the triumph of Christianity, but he also knew the Roman Empire as the fullest historical embodiment of that City of Man that is the opposite of the City of God; but that City of Man is dialectically necessary to the City of God, and necessary both to its apocalyptic and to its historical triumph.

Did Christianity triumph because it knew and embodied an absolute darkness far deeper than any darkness known by the ancient world? Inevitably, Christianity was truly repulsive to the pagan mind, truly known as an assault upon the world itself, and nothing could be more alien to the ancient world than a Christian understanding of sin, one vastly distancing Christianity from every pagan understanding of salvation or of life, but equally distancing Christianity from every pagan understanding of redemption. So it is that the "bad conscience" that Nietzsche knows as a terrifying curse was introduced into the world by Christianity, a bad conscience apart from which no Christian forgiveness of sin is possible, but Christianity can know that forgiveness as redemption itself; hence, this is a forgiveness wholly different from that forgiveness that we commonly know, and is so as a profound offense. Just as the forgiveness of sin was the most offensive of the acts of Jesus, and one that justly could be known as an ultimate blasphemy, the forgiveness of sin is an assault upon any possible righteousness, or any possible innocence. For the absolute Yes-saying of this forgiveness of sin is simultaneously an absolute No-saying, and apart from that No-saying it is wholly unreal, here is a grace that is grace and judgment at once, and an absolute grace that is an absolute judgment.

Can we know such a judgment as occurring in our world? How could this be possible if a bad conscience is apparently weaker today than ever previously in our history? Could this ending be a consequence of the ending of self-consciousness itself, and an ending that is not simply a dissolution of self-consciousness, but far rather a transformation of self-consciousness into what Kierkegaard knew as a total objectivity, and a total objectivity that he can know as the pure reversal of all genuine subjectivity? If a Kierkegaardian subjectivity is truly unknowable today, could that be the inevitable consequence of the realization of what he understood as a process of total objectification, and a total objectification of subjectivity itself? But then judgment itself, so far from occurring as an interior judgment, could be occurring as that very objectification. Inevitably, a bad conscience would disappear, or rather would wholly be transformed, and transformed into a world in which no real or actual conscience would be possible, or none that could have an impact upon its own world. Then guilt itself would wholly be transformed, disappearing as an interior guilt, but being reborn in an awesomely alien world, and alien not only in its absolute exteriority, but in its absolute emptiness, for just as Augustine can know sin as the incarnation of nothingness, we can know our new world as an incarnation of nothingness, a nothingness far more actual than any nothingness that Augustine or Christian scholasticism could know.

Augustine most deeply differs from his Plotinian or Neoplatonic ground in knowing an actuality of nothingness, an actuality of nothingness that is the actuality of sin, and even if sin can ontologically be known as nothingness, it is nevertheless overwhelmingly real in the fallen will, and that will comprehends everything that we can know as history. Certainly an Augustinian could understand our new world as a full embodiment of the "City of Man," a "City of Man" that is eternally predestined to Hell, and one fully displaying the marks of that predestination, marks that are decisive signs of the absolute judgment of God. That judgment occurs simultaneously with God's redemption, for the "City of Man" and the "City of God" have parallel histories, histories culminating in a final and apocalyptic judgment, but an apocalyptic judgment that is inseparable from an apocalyptic redemption. It is impossible to know that redemption without knowing that judgment, and the saints can know that judgment even in Heaven, a knowledge apart from which they could not be "saints." So that if an eternal Hell is truly necessary to a uniquely Christian Heaven, or an absolute damnation absolutely necessary to a uniquely Christian redemption, then an absolutely alien totality is absolutely necessary to the totality of grace, a grace that in being ubiquitous or everywhere, is everywhere as judgment and redemption simultaneously.

Nietzsche's own roots were deeply Lutheran, and no theologian knows sin so purely as does Luther, and if this is a knowledge essential to Luther's radical understanding of justification, we can understand this justification as being reborn in Nietzsche's revolutionary enactment of Eternal Recurrence. Luther's only full theological treatise, *The Bondage of the Will*, is a pure enactment of predestination, a predestination that is reborn in the eternal predestination of Eternal Recurrence. Just as Luther can know the Yes-saying of grace only through the No-saying of damnation, Nietzsche can know the absolute Yes-saying of Eternal Recurrence only through an absolute No-saying to everything whatsoever, or to everything whatsoever that is not Eternal Recurrence. Nietzsche's Eternal Recurrence is an absolute affirmation, and an absolute affirmation of even the most horrible evil, therefore it is a transfiguration of evil, a transfiguration occurring in the willing of the totality of all and everything, a willing that is the Will to Power, and just thereby a willing of what Augustine knows as the Will of God. Moreover, Eternal Recurrence is a truly apocalyptic totality, one only possible as the consequence of the deepest and most ultimate ending, the ending of everything that we have known as history, an ending ushering in an absolute nihilism, but that is the very nihilism in which Eternal Recurrence is enacted, a nihilism absolutely essential to Eternal Recurrence, and absolutely essential as an absolute ending.

Just as Nietzsche knows nihilism more profoundly than any other thinker, this is a nihilism that he knows as a fully dawning historical actuality, one that he foresees as being fully incarnate in our world. If that world embodies an ultimate ending, it embodies an ultimate beginning as well, an absolute beginning that is inseparable from an absolute ending, and yet an absolute beginning that is a pure and total grace. Nietzsche and Hegel are alone among philosophers in knowing a pure and total redemption, but Nietzsche knows an apocalyptic ending as Hegel does not, an ending of everything that Hegel knows as philosophy, and only that ending makes possible a knowledge of Eternal Recurrence, or makes possible absolute Yes-saying itself. That Yes-saying is an eternally predestined Yes-saying; indeed, it is eternal predestination itself, and a double predestination of an absolute evil and an absolute good at once, as for the first time predestination is fully and comprehensively enacted, and comprehensively enacted as actuality itself. If only the death of God makes possible this enactment, this enactment was never previously possible, but with the full occurrence of the death of God, the enactment of Eternal Recurrence is not only possible but inevitable, and inevitable as an absolutely necessary transfiguration of that absolute nothingness that the death of God releases. That transfiguration embodies an absolute joy, and a joy only possible by way of a transfiguration of this nothingness, so that an absolute nothingness is essential to this absolute joy, just as an absolute evil is essential to a uniquely Christian redemption.

All too significantly, Nietzsche is our only thinker of a pure and total forgiveness of sin, a thinking that in enacting Eternal Recurrence enacts that forgiveness, and enacts it as a pure redemption, a redemption occurring in the Yes-saying of Eternal Recurrence, and occurring in that Yes-saying that reverses a total No-saying, and reverses that absolute No-saying that Nietzsche knows as the uniquely Christian God. In *The Antichrist*, he draws forth a Jesus who is the only precursor of his own Zarathustra, a Jesus continually enacting a total forgiveness, a Jesus absolutely removed from everything that we know as history, but above all a Jesus who is infinitely distant from the Christian God, and the very opposite of everything that we have known as Christianity. In this last will and testament, and one even more a testament and will than *Ecce Homo*, Paul is the ultimate enemy, a Paul whom Nietzsche could know as the creator of Christianity, and the creator of an absolute guilt and *ressentiment*. That is a guilt that is a true opposite of the praxis of Jesus, one absolutely reversing Jesus himself, and a reversal of that reversal can and will only occur in the death of God, the most ultimate event that has ever occurred, and one bringing history itself to an end. No thinker has thought that ending more deeply than did Nietzsche, and he finally knows it as an absolutely joyous event, an event that is the true gospel, a gospel reversing that *dysangel* that is the Christian gospel, but a gospel only possible as the consequence of a final ending.

But if Eternal Recurrence is a genuine redemption, and a redemption that is the transfiguration of evil, and therefore the transfiguration of sin, is not Eternal Recurrence an enactment of a uniquely Christian atonement, and one only possible within a uniquely Christian horizon? And if *Thus Spoke Zarathustra* enacts a truly new vision of the body, and one in which "body" is all in all, is such a body possible apart from an ultimate incarnation, an incarnation in which "Spirit" realizes itself as body and as body alone? And if this is possible only through the death of God, is that death not an absolutely atoning death, but now a death fully and wholly coincident with actuality itself? While there is certainly an Hegelian ground in such an understanding of atonement, now every possible "idealism" has wholly disappeared, and disappeared in a total epiphany of body itself, as for the first time we are given a genuine vision of the resurrection of the body. If such a resurrection is a total transfiguration of sin, it could only be a dialectical transfiguration, one only possible in the depths of sin or darkness, and only possible in a horizon in which those depths are all in all. Now death itself undergoes its most awesome epiphany or realization, and now only a willing, and an absolute willing, of that death make possible such a transfiguration, one that could only be a willing of the death of God, which alone makes possible an atonement that *is* resurrection. If Hegel could never think resurrection, or think an actual resurrection, that could well be because Hegel could never think the body itself, and if at no other point is Hegel more coincident with the history of philosophy as a whole, at no other point is he more distant from Nietzsche.

Yes, Nietzsche is the most anti-philosophical of all philosophers, and even more profoundly anti-philosophical than Kierkegaard himself, but is this not a theological necessity, and a theological necessity in a post-Hegelian world? Nietzsche and Kierkegaard can be understood as a dialectical polarity, each the very opposite of the other, and yet each created an absolutely individual thinking, one truly paralleled in no other thinkers, but a uniquely individual thinking ultimately embodying their worlds, and embodying the interior depths of those worlds as does no other thinking. Kierkegaard underwent his second conversion or "metamorphosis" only when he finally came to realize that God had *forgotten* his sin, and then wrote *The Sickness Unto Death*, whose dialectical thesis is that sin is the opposite of faith, but an opposite only realized in the depths of the forgiveness of sin. Those interior depths that Kierkegaard and Nietzsche most purely and most comprehensively draw forth are interior depths that either perish or are wholly transfigured in that very realization, and perish in a total forgiveness or a total transfiguration of those very depths, a transfiguration in which these depths become the very opposite of themselves. Kierkegaard could never think redemption itself, or not think it apart from his edifying discourses, and yet Nietzsche finally thinks redemption and redemption alone, and if this is a redemption from the ultimate depths of an absolute No-saying, this is a redemption from what Kierkegaard, too, could know as the absolute No-saying of God, but a wrath of God inseparable from the grace of God, even as Nietzsche's absolute Yes-saying is inseparable from an absolute No-saying.

Chapter Five

A Calling

The Body of Christ

There has been no greater challenge and genuine curse to all established Christianity than the modern historical consciousness, a uniquely modern historical consciousness, one that has wholly transformed everything that we can understand as the Bible, and given us revolutionary understandings of both a new and an old Israel. Nietzsche could know the "slave revolt of morality" as a pure inversion of every archaic morality, but it alone made possible the survival of Israel in face of the catastrophe of the first exile. Israel is the only people ever to have survived such a catastrophe, a survival possible only by way of the creation of a truly new faith and a truly new people, for Israel, in losing its land, its monarchy, and its cultus and priesthood, lost every ground of life in the ancient world. But monarchic Israel itself was a new Israel, and twentieth century scholarship has demonstrated that the Torah, or the greater body of the Bible, was created by monarchic Israel, if not by post-monarchic Israel, so that the perishing of monarchic Israel was an ultimate event, and one leading to a truly new Israel. No such absolute transformation had previously occurred in history, as every given ground of life and existence is wholly transformed, then everything that Nietzsche could know as a "noble morality" becomes impossible, and a people is born whose life is truly independent of everything whatsoever that had previously been known or manifest as ultimate ground. Hence a true Israel is born in exile, and the true Abraham or the true Moses is a post-exilic founder, only in exile does Israel become a truly unique people, and only thereby is Israel truly "chosen" by Yahweh.

Christianity, however, knows itself as the new Israel, although it predominantly does so by way of the royal sovereignty, the cultic priesthood, and the messianic consciousness of monarchic Israel, even knowing God Himself as absolute monarch and an absolutely monarchic Lord, and the Son of God as the messianic ruler descended from King David, a King David now known as King Jesus, and a King Jesus presiding over that new monarchic and cultic kingdom that is the Church. If thereby we can know a dominant Christianity as an ultimate regression from the historical new Israel, it is simultaneously and even thereby, a reversal of its own original ground, and the only real precedent of this absolute transformation of Christianity is that absolute transformation of Israel that occurred through exile. But these are transformations moving in truly opposing or opposite directions, Israel losing or abandoning every actual mode of archaic existence, and every possibility of monarchy or lordship, and Christianity transforming an apocalyptic movement into an archaic or primordial movement of eternal return, and itself evolving into the greatest empire in history. Of course, there were Jewish movements that were monarchic movements in post-exilic Israel, but these wholly perished in that second exile effected by the Roman Empire, an exile playing a decisive role in the transformation of Christianity, and one that New Testament scholars can know as having had an ultimate impact upon the New Testament itself.

Thus it is now possible to know ultimate transformations as being embodied in the Bible, and ultimate historical transformations, transformations truly paralleled nowhere else in history, except insofar as these occur in later historical trans- formations, and later historical transformations at this crucial point in genuine historical continuity with the Bible. But these are transformations that all established theological thinking refuses, and most so in our contemporary world, and if the established discipline of theology is now more conservative than it has ever previously been, here lies a gulf between our theological world and the great theological breakthroughs of an Augustine or an Aquinas, and in this perspective theology has quite literally come to an end. Could this be an ending comparable to the ending of an old Israel? Surely the perishing of Christendom parallels the perishing of monarchic Israel, and if it was revolutionary prophets of Israel who made possible the rebirth and renewal of Israel, could there be prophets in our world who could make possible the rebirth and renewal of Christianity? Just as post-exilic scribes and priests created a new Bible and a new Israel, and did so in large measure under the impact of the prophetic revolution, is that a possibility in our new world? If so, it must be understood that this could occur only by way of a total and even an absolute transformation, but nevertheless such an absolute transformation would be in genuine continuity with Israel, and in genuine continuity with an actual and historical Israel, an Israel inseparable from everything that Christianity knows as the Bible.

We must never forget that neo-orthodox theology was born only by way of an ever fuller phenomenological suspension or reduction of every possible critical or historical understanding of the Bible. This reduction becomes indistinguishable from a fundamentalist refusal of Biblical scholarship, and it is now all too clear that a genuinely Biblical theology could only be a truly revolutionary theology, as most manifest in the opposing perspective of everything that has become manifest as orthodox theology. There is a major body of Biblical scholarship that knows the Book of Deuteronomy as the most revolutionary book in the Bible, a book "discovered" in the course of a reform by King Josiah of Judah in the late seventh century BCE, hence occurring after the destruction of the more powerful kingdom of Israel, a discovery soon creating a truly if not an absolutely new Moses, a new Moses revealing a new Torah, but now the last book of the Pentateuch becomes the first book, and a "first" book generating or transforming the other books, as a truly new Torah is revealed, and now one comprehending and transforming the major historical books of the Bible, as a truly new Bible is a consequence of this reformation. Even the creation of the New Testament pales in the face of this ultimate transformation, and it is a post-apocalyptic Christianity rather than a post-exilic Judaism that is most drawn to a monarchic Bible, a monarchic Bible in which Torah as "law" is absolute, for Christianity has never been able to absorb anything that Judaism knows as Torah. Nietzsche can speak of the joining of the Old Testament and the New Testament as the most ultimate desecration that has ever occurred, as a truly noble book is united with its very opposite, and certainly the Christian Old Testament if only thereby is vastly removed from the Torah of Israel, but nevertheless the uniquely Christian God echoes the new absolutism of the Book of Deuteronomy, and precisely so in His new and absolute sovereignty.

All too ironically, only a generation after the discovery of the Book of Deuteronomy in the Temple in Jerusalem the shrunken and politically insignificant kingdom of Judah perishes, so that the dominical language of this new Torah calling for a pure and total kingdom of God is almost immediately reversed by historical actuality itself. The Book of Deuteronomy is the most radically judgmental book of the Bible, promising terrible curses to a rebellious Israel, and comparable curses to the enemies of Israel, and it seems to foresee an immediate judgment of Israel when it declares that even if you are exiled to the ends of the world, from there the Lord your God will gather you back, making you more prosperous and numerous than your ancestors, and will circumcise your heart so that you will love the Lord with all your heart in order that you may live (30:4-6). The Deuteronomic reformation can be understood not simply as the renewal of an old covenant but as a genuine transformation of that covenant, and if this made possible the very birth of what we know as the Bible in exilic Israel, that Bible is the consequence of an ultimate historical transformation.

This is the perspective in which we must view the profound historical transformations of Christianity, but have these transformations now come to an end, or could an ultimate historical transformation of Christianity now be occurring that is truly invisible to us, one apparently unheard in our contemporary churches, and yet nevertheless one that is truly real? The Pauline image of the body of Christ has itself undergone an enormous transformation in Christian history, one already beginning in the Pauline epistles themselves, and while this image fundamentally evokes that new world or new æon created by the Crucifixion (Romans 7:4 and I Corinthians 1:22), in Ephesians and Colossians it calls forth that new Church of which Christ is the head, and while it is highly questionable whether these are genuinely Pauline epistles, this is the image of the body of Christ that ever more comprehensively dominated Christianity, and one ever more fully establishing a chasm between the body of Christ and the body of humanity as a whole, just as it establishes a gulf between the body of Christ and the very actuality of body itself. No such gulf between body and grace is manifest in the Hebrew Bible, but it is overwhelming in the greater body of Christianity, and is so most fully in that very Christianity that is at war with the world, and most at war with its own internal heretics, heretics themselves ultimately divided between those committed to the very dissolution of the body and those committed to an ultimate transfiguration of the body, a transfiguration inseparable from an absolutely new world.

Paul knows a genuine distinction between "body" (*soma*) and "flesh" *(sarx.)* While "flesh" is sin itself, "body" is a vehicle of grace, and the vehicle of an apocalyptic and hence absolutely transfiguring grace, a grace truly reversed in that ultimate transformation of Christianity beginning to occur immediately after Paul, one already present in those Pauline epistles produced by disciples of Paul, and then one fully overwhelming in virtually all of patristic Christian literature and life. Nor is this Christian transformation of the body truly challenged until the Gothic revolution, and nothing is more revealing of that revolution than the discovery of the body itself, one manifest in the cathedral sculpture of the twelfth century. While this sculpture evolved out of Romanesque sculpture, a decisive break now occurs, a break issuing in the Christian advent of the whole and integral human body. Suddenly the body fully breaks forth in Gothic sculpture, as for the first time in Christian history the body can now stand forth and be fully actual as a truly human and natural body, for even if a resurrection of the body in Christian art now only partially occurs, it is real nonetheless, and real even as a sensuous presence. Most startling of all, Christ himself appears incarnate in the body in the sculpture of *Christ Teaching* in the south portal of Chartres Cathedral, carved about 1215. Not only is this a bodily Christ, but also a fully human Christ, a Christ now appearing as the very antithesis of the Christ of Glory who had dominated Byzantine and even Romanesque art. Now the Incarnation is actualized in the Christian consciousness as an incarnation in the body, and the human body itself can now for the first time stand forth and be real as the body of Christ.

Gothic cathedral statuary is the first Christian art to portray the human body as being fully natural and truly holy at once. The Gothic cathedrals themselves embody a truly transfiguring power, as that infinite light that now dawns becomes embodied in the eye that beholds it, and the Eye of Christ is no longer an infinitely distant point upon our horizon, but far rather an Eye that now sees in our own. Yet the very glory of this radically new vision is dialectically inseparable from an ultimately new vision of the crucified Christ. Whereas the Byzantine Christ is predominantly if not wholly the Christ of Glory or the Pantocrater, this is the Christ who initially appears in Western medieval art. In the late tenth century the crucified Christ is carved in wood in the *Gero Crucifix* in the Cologne Cathedral. This is probably the oldest monumental crucifix in Europe. A distinctive sign of the dead Christ on the Cross is that his eyes are closed, as are the eyes in the *Gero Crucifix*, and the dead eyes accompany a truly dead and broken body, a Christ who is fully the Christ of Passion. Only over the course of a millennium does the crucified Christ actually enter Christian art, and the Christ of majesty is not shattered in Western Christian art until the late fourteenth century. Only in Gothic art is Christ both fully human and fully divine, and only in that art is his body both a glorious and a sacrificial body, a body that is the Christ of Glory and the Christ of Passion at once, as fully manifest in the most revolutionary of all Christian painters, Giotto.

It is impossible to doubt that a genuine revolution occurs in Christian art, and in Christian poetry, too, a revolution that is not only an imaginative revolution, but one ever more fully occurring in Christian society, as manifest in the progressive growth of a new freedom, a new freedom embodying a truly new future, a new future that is a truly apocalyptic and total future, as gloriously embodied in the *Commedia*. Dante inaugurated a uniquely Christian poetry, as an ultimately new epic is fully born, one integrating every domain whatsoever. For the first time in the Christian world a truly total vision is born, but that vision is a genuinely apocalyptic vision, and as such a revolutionary vision, a revolutionary vision that is a truly heterodox vision, and Dante is the only major artist who was condemned by the Papacy. Yet, after his death Catholicism ever more fully sanctioned Dante as its ultimate and most sacred poet, thus demonstrating once again how Christian heresy can pass into Christian orthodoxy, a process already beginning with Paul, and if thereby we can understand how heresy and orthodoxy are integrally related in Christianity, this is inseparable from an ultimately forward movement in Christianity, and a forward movement occurring by way of an ultimate transformation.

Great outbursts of creativity in Christianity have inevitably been succeeded by periods of reversal and decline. If we can know the nineteenth century as giving us our most revolutionary transformation of Christianity, one truly real both in imaginative vision and in pure thinking, this revolution is accompanied by a progressive collapse or disintegration of Christian society, one that Kierkegaard could know as a pure objectification of interiority and faith, but one that becomes far more overwhelming in the twentieth century, a century posing the most ultimate challenge that Christianity has ever faced. Christianity is truly invisible in the major cultural expressions of the twentieth century or, if not wholly invisible, is manifest therein only in its most radical expressions. These occur in the most creative and challenging embodiments of the twentieth century imagination and, as opposed to the nineteenth century, never fully occur in thinking itself, and certainly not in a twentieth century theology, which despite its initial power thereafter becomes ever more fully retrogressive and reactionary. The French Revolution is surely one source of this reaction, and if it released the first comprehensively reactionary movement in Europe, this is one that truly transformed the Church. Thereafter, the Church for the first time becomes comprehensively sectarian, and only then does Christianity become fully realized as a movement of ultimate and eternal return.

But is that ultimate return inevitably inseparable from its very opposite? Just as innumerable theologians have proclaimed that modern science is a consequence of Christianity, could that which is seemingly most opposed to Christianity at bottom be an expression of Christianity itself? Certainly so if one accepts a Blakean vision of an apocalyptic identity of Satan and Christ, but could that vision be anything more than the purest fantasy, and a fantasy wholly removed from any possible actuality, or any possible history or world? Or is it possible that an absolutely new world truly has dawned in our world and history, one that is the very opposite of everything that is now openly manifest as Christianity, and above all the opposite of everything that is historically manifest as the uniquely Christian God? The deep emptiness of our new world is truly revealing at this point, a pure and yet total emptiness that our poets have embodied and enacted as an absolute nothingness, a nothingness vastly different from any pre-modern epiphany of nothingness, and yet a nothingness that we can know as being inseparable from actuality itself. The first pure vision of this nothingness occurs in *Moby Dick*, and if we can know the White Whale as a uniquely modern enactment of the Christian God, and one giving us a *horror religiosus* going far beyond that alien transcendence that Hegel and Kierkegaard could know, this epic enactment is surely a premonition of the horrors of our century. But, so, too, is it a genuine vision of the absolute nothingness of the Godhead, yet now an absolutely alien nothingness, and a nothingness consuming everything in its wake.

If only through the White Whale we can know an image of the very body of Satan, a Satan that is a truly Blakean Satan, a Satan that is pure transcendence itself, and an absolutely alien transcendence. Here is perhaps our purest image of that *mysterium tremendum* that is liberated from any possible *mysterium fascinans*, an absolute judgment occurring apart from any possible grace, and if thereby Melville is truly a forerunner of a uniquely twentieth century imagination, he is so precisely as a visionary of Satan. Yet if the White Whale is truly a vision of the body of Satan, does it foreclose every possible vision of the body of Christ within its horizon, or does it make possible truly new visions of the body of Christ, visions of a crucified body that is all in all, or a crucified body that is body itself? Certainly this would be a reversal of the first millennium of Christian history, but is it a reversal or a fulfillment of the second millennium of that history, a millennium culminating in both a pure vision and a pure thinking of the Crucified God, a crucified God that is truly the body of Christ? Could that body be an emptying of everything that is given us as body itself, an emptying of every body that is immediately and integrally our own? Just as ancient Christianity could know that body as a consequence of original sin, could a truly new Christianity know that body as a primal site of the sacrificial body of Christ?

While images of the Christ of Glory ever more fully disintegrate in the West with the very advent of modernity, images of the Christ of Passion not only become ever more comprehensive, but ever more progressively undergo an ultimate transformation, finally disappearing, or virtually disappearing, as overt or open images of Christ, and doing so by embodying a truly new and anonymous totality, as luminously manifest in the deeper imaginative enactments of the twentieth century. Surely *Finnegans Wake* is a primal expression of these enactments, but no other literary work since Rabelais has given us such a primal expression of body itself. Now body truly is a total body, and a total body enacting a universal sacrifice, or a *Missa Jubilaea*, a sacrifice that is cosmic and historical at once, and one embodied in this truly new vision of the body of Christ. Now the body of Christ is not only a universal body, but a truly kenotic or sacrificial body. Only now does that sacrificial body become all in all, and yet it is all in all as an immediate actuality, an actuality enacting us in this very universal sacrifice, and not enacting our "soul," but rather enacting our body itself, a body far deeper and far more ultimate than anything that is manifest as our given body. Not only is this an epic enactment of the transfiguration of the body, but as opposed to every previous image of the resurrection of the body, this is a transfiguration occurring in the brute actuality of the body itself, for paradoxically it is *Finnegans Wake* that is our most realistic novel or epic, as most clearly manifest in that ultimately new body that is here called forth.

Joyce is perhaps the most deeply Biblical writer of the twentieth century, and is thereby in genuine continuity with the Christian epic tradition, a literary tradition that is more openly and more fully a Biblical tradition than is any other, yet a tradition that has transformed itself more profoundly than any other literary tradition. This can be understood as a consequence of the Bible itself. Although Dante had the deepest impact upon Joyce, Joyce himself could know Blake as his purest predecessor, for Joyce is truly Blakean in the very universality of his enactment of Satan, and in *Ulysses* Satan falls and yet knows no fall—*Lucifer, dico, qui nescit occasum* (50)—a fall that becomes a total fall in *Finnegans Wake*. That very fall is comprehensively enacted in the *Wake*, one beginning on its very first page and continuing throughout our first epic of the body itself. But Joyce goes far beyond Blake in his universal enactment of Satan. Now Satan is embodied in the depths of bodily actuality, and there embodied in a continual and a universal sacrifice or crucifixion of "Haar Faagher," a sacrifice finally culminating in Book Four in the resurrection of Anna Livia Plurabelle. Now true bodily actuality is a truly sacrificial actuality, and sacrifice for the first time is enacted in the fullness of that actuality. Therefore, this is a body that can be known as the body of Christ, and not only the body of that broken Christ who is the Christ of Passion, but also the body of the resurrected Christ, for just as Blake named and enacted the resurrected Christ as Jerusalem, Joyce names and enacts resurrection itself as Anna Livia Plurabelle.

Molly Bloom is the earlier epiphany and enactment of Anna Livia Plurabelle. If Molly's final monologue in *Ulysses* is our only enactment of an ultimate joy that is a genuinely and fully realistic enactment, this occurs in the full actuality of Molly's body, and while unlike Anna's this is not a sacrificial body, it is a body of bliss, even an ecstatic bliss, and the final Yes of Molly is an ultimate Yes-saying to the body itself. Can that be an enactment of the resurrection of the body, and a resurrection not in the beyond, but in the here and now, one wholly reversing what has been given to us as resurrection, and certainly reversing every possible "spiritual" resurrection? Could it precisely thereby be a recovery of an apocalyptic resurrection that historical Christianity has wholly reversed? Joyce is the greatest of all blasphemers, even surpassing Nietzsche himself as an ultimate blasphemer. Is he most blasphemous in his very enactments of resurrection, and therefore most blasphemous in his enactments of the body of Christ? Now that body as a crucified body *is* a resurrected body, and while this enactment is primal in Paul and the Fourth Gospel, it is wholly alien to the great body of Christianity, and is not recovered in vision until the fullness of the modern world. Then it occurs only in our most revolutionary vision, a revolutionary vision seemingly reversing the New Testament itself, but nevertheless fully embodying a New Testament Christianity in that reversal, and above all so in its vision of a total body that is the apocalyptic body of Christ.

Absolute Nothingness

One of the deeper mysteries of the Christian world, if not its deepest mystery, is the mystery of nothingness itself, a nothingness that is both illusory and real, illusory as an ontological nothingness, yet real as sin and death, and above all so as an eternal death. A real or an actual nothingness does not enter philosophical thinking until German Idealism, then it makes possible that absolute negation that Hegel so profoundly enacts, just as it makes possible the first philosophical understanding of evil, or the first philosophical understanding of a real and actual evil. While such an understanding is implicit in Augustine's truly new understanding of sin, Augustine's Neoplatonism foreclosed the possibility of a philosophical understanding of that pure negativity, and at this point not even an Aquinas could transcend such a Neoplatonism. This transcendence does not fully occur historically until

Luther, and then it occurs only by way of an ending of philosophical theology itself, an ending deeply renewed by Barth in the twentieth century, a Barth who could know the triumph of Christ as an ultimate and final ending of the Nihil, a Nihil that is real if only in that ending (*Church Dogmatics* III, 3). Not until Barth does a major theologian speak of the Nihil or the Nothing, a language only possible after the collapse of Christian scholasticism, and this occurs in a new world in which there is an ultimate epiphany of evil and nothingness, one culminating in the Holocaust. In the wake of that Holocaust could it be anything but a pure blasphemy to speak of evil as the privation of the good?

Goethe's *Faust* is that imaginative work that had the greatest impact upon the modern German mind, a mind that gave us our first philosophical understanding of an actual nothingness. If the Faust myth was born in the very advent of modernity, it enacts a uniquely Western damnation, a damnation that is the consequence of the will to power, and a damnation that Goethe gave his deepest power to reversing. This occurs in the second part of Goethe's ultimate drama, as the passionately subjective Faust of the first part ever more fully realizes a trans-subjective and trans-individual power, a power that alone can reverse the damnation of Faust. This most decisively occurs in the first act of the tragedy's second part, occurring in a descent into the realm of the Mothers in "Dark Gallery." Mephistopheles reveals to Faust that these goddesses are enthroned in sublime solitude, a solitude where there is neither space nor time. Indeed, there is no way to this solitude, a solitude that is a pure void, and one that Mephistopheles identifies as the Nothing. Faust accepts a summons to this Nothing, and can even declare: "In deinem Nichts hoff ich das All zu finden," I hope to find the All in your Nothing (6256). For if that All is truly the Nothing of Mephistopheles or of Satan, a realization of that All will be a triumphant fulfillment of the wager in the first part (1692-1706), and a fulfillment reversing the damnation of Faust. Now a descent occurs into the unbound realms of form, realms that have long since been dissipated, and a descent that Mephistopheles can identity with ascent. Only when Faust has arrived in the deepest abyss will he behold the radiant glow of the Mothers, and then encounter that ultimate transformation that is eternal re-creation. As Faust declares, the Mothers have their throne in boundlessness, a boundlessness that is the womb of all and everything, and a boundlessness that is the final destiny of Faust.

This destiny is enacted in the conclusion of the drama, when Faust as Faust disappears, and disappears by way of an ultimate union with the Eternal Feminine, an Eternal Feminine that is a resolution of those deep feminine powers occurring throughout the drama, but that are only unveiled in Faust's descent into the realm of the Mothers. These powers are embodied in the Catholic Mother of God, who is here the one source of salvation in the Christian world, and even as the conclusion of *Faust* is a renewal and reenactment of the conclusion of the *Paradiso*, the Mothers are here the one source of salvation, Mothers that are the primal source of the Virgin and Beatrice alike, and that is the very source that is ecstatically celebrated in the poetry that concludes the drama. This is an ultimate hymn of celebration, intoned by the *chorus mysticus*, celebrating that "Ewig-Weibliche" or Eternal Feminine drawing us to an absolutely primordial transcendence, a primordial transcendence that is an absolute transfiguration of nothingness itself: "Das Unzulaengliche, hier wird's Ereignis." Now what is truly empty or deficient or nothing finally becomes *Ereignis*, a holy and disembodied action that is the action of the redeemed Faust.

Not until Heidegger is that *Ereignis* philosophically reborn, a Heidegger who along with Sartre is alone as a twentieth century philosopher speaking of the Nothing, and a Heidegger who knows an apocalyptic epiphany of *Ereignis* occurring in the very heart of darkness. Only in the posthumously published *Beiträge* does Heidegger give us a full exposition of *Ereignis*. Here, Being itself is finally known as *Ereignis*, and known as such against the transcendent God of Christianity, an *Ereignis* that is "originary history." But only now is that history realizing its fullness, and realizing it in the advent of the utmost remoteness of the "last god," one bringing history to its end.

No redemption occurs here, but rather a *letting-into* (*Einsetzung*), a releasement of the originarily ownmost in Being itself. Now the empowering of man to God's necessity becomes manifest, and *Ereignis* comes into the open (413). An ultimate struggle occurs throughout this work, and far more so than in any other work of Heidegger's, and here he can say that Being has the character of nothing (*nichthaft*), for Being needs the *not* to last for the steadfastness of its truth, and that means that it needs the *opposition* of all that is nothing, the "not-being" (101). There is a deep emphasis here upon the abandonment of Being, one that first happened in Christianity and its absolutely transcendent God, an abandonment in which Being abandons beings, but this abandonment is the fundamental event of our history, and one that is now being reversed in the apocalyptic advent of *Ereignis*.

Surely such an *Ereignis* is inseparable from an absolute nothingness, as first fully enacted in the second part of *Faust*. Theologians have known both Goethe and Heidegger as being profoundly pagan, and most manifestly so in their very invocation of "the gods." Heidegger is thereby unique among our philosophers, but would it be possible for Heidegger fully to speak of *Ereignis* apart from speaking of the "last god"? And is that "last god" knowable apart from the depths of nothingness itself, or is *Ereignis* possible apart from an ultimate opposition, an opposition that can only finally be the opposition of an absolute nothingness; and, is that the absolute nothingness that Christianity first named as Satan? The truth is that there is very little actual thinking of Satan in Christianity. Imaginatively, Satan is not fully envisioned until the advent of the modern world. Then, not only does Satanic imagery abound, but a thinking becomes comprehensive that the theologian can know as a Satanic thinking, and above all so in its enactment of the death of God. Theologically, that enactment can be known as the enactment of nothingness itself, and of an absolute nothingness, an enactment most openly occurring in Nietzsche's proclamation of the death of God, but one no less occurring in imaginative voyages into an absolute nothingness, which would appear to be the very signature of a late modern imagination. Is that a signature that we can know in the advent of postmodernity itself? Could our new emptiness be a reflection of an absolute nothingness, but now a nothingness that is actuality itself?

Hegel's *Science of Logic* can know a pure being that is identical with pure nothingness, and this identification is the consequence of an absolute beginning, for if it belongs to the very nature of this beginning that it must be being and nothing else, that beginning in its very identify as beginning is the unity of being and nothing, a unity in which being and nothing are distinguished in the beginning. This is a distinction that is absolutely essential to beginning itself, for the beginning as such is only on the way to being, a being that is the "other" of non-being. Only non-being is the other of being, and therefore the being embodied in the beginning is a being that removes itself from non-being, or that negates non-being as something opposed to and other than itself. That negation is genesis or the beginning, and therefore the opposites of being and non-being are united in that beginning, a beginning that is the undifferentiated unity of being and nothing. But absolute beginning embodies mediation within itself, and a mediation that is known or manifest in the knowledge that being *is* nothing. This occurs in the realization that pure being, or being without any further differentiation, or that being that is the indeterminate immediate, is in fact "nothing." It is a wholly empty intuition that presents us with the thought of pure being and pure nothing, and that is an emptiness in which pure nothing is the same as pure being, and it is the vanishing of that pure being and that pure nothing that is the advent of becoming.

Never was Hegel more purely dialectical than in this purely logical enactment, but this is a logical enactment betraying the ultimate impact of a new world, one that has already left Christendom wholly behind, and also one that has truly transcended or deconstructed the Western ontological tradition. Not only has every possible Western metaphysics now been ended, but it has been ended through a realization of that nothing that is the opposite of being, and if it is Hegel's philosophy alone that fully calls forth this nothing, it is a purely dialectical thinking that most fully knows nothingness itself. Not until

Schelling and Hegel is an actual nothingness known philosophically, but that knowledge can be understood as having a uniquely Christian ground, and a uniquely Christian ground in the apprehension of an absolute negation. The *Science of Logic* begins with the judgment that immediacy and mediation are inseparable, and the apparent opposition between them is a nullity, a nullity that is the actuality of consciousness itself. That nullity is the reversal of a primordial nothing, so that "nothing" itself is now inseparable from being, a nothing that has now ceased to be an abstract or inactual nothing. However, that perishing is not a simple perishing, it is far rather the preservation and transcendence of a primordial nothing in an actual nothing that is united with being. At no point is the *Science of Logic* more original than in its creation of the purely logical category of an actual nothing, a nothing that is the consequence of genesis itself, or of that absolute beginning that is an absolute negation.

Hegel can conclude the initial essay in the *Science of Logic* on "With What Must the Science Begin?" with the remark that God has the absolutely undisputed right that the beginning be made with Him. But this is immediately followed by an insistence that in the science of logic the absolute or God is in the beginning "only an empty word." That empty word is realized in the very beginning of thinking, a thinking that knows "only being," and therefore the content of that thinking is only an empty or inactual word. Thus actuality begins with the emptiness of a being that is "only being," and even if this emptiness embodies an actual potentiality for the world, it nevertheless is an actual emptiness, and an actual emptiness that will resolve itself into that being that *is* nothing. Accordingly, this is a "beginning" that is the beginning of bare immediacy, and even if that is a mediated immediacy, and mediated by an empty if actual consciousness, beginning itself and even absolute beginning or genesis is the beginning of an actual emptiness. Hegel thereby reverses every traditional Christian understanding of the creation, for creation out of nothing cannot be a creation out of a primordial emptiness or void, but far rather creation out of an actual emptiness or an actual nothingness, thereby making philosophically possible that fundamental Augustinian understanding that evil or the deficiency of being derives from our having been created from nothing (*City of God*, XII, 6).

Evil can be understood as the most challenging of all philosophical and theological questions, and most so when it is identified with "non-being," and it is all too significant that there is virtually no attempt to meet this challenge in twentieth century philosophy, Levinas alone attempts this, but this is just the point at which his thinking is most abbreviated and most fragmentary. Of course, theologians revel in their understanding of sin, but this is never conjoined with an understanding of absolute evil, or even with an understanding of evil itself, for evil is not only the great unanswered question theologically, but the most forbidden one as well. And it is most forbidden because if it is deeply asked it must be asked of God Himself, and the real theological question is not why does God permit evil, but is evil itself inseparable from God, one that is potentially answered in the traditional theological answer that God permits evil to make possible the freedom of the will, for that is inevitably an affirmation that the fullness of God's creation, or the fullness of God's eternal acts, is inseparable from an ultimate realization of evil. Hegel is alone among our primal thinkers in actually thinking the evil of God, and while Hegel is Augustinian in understanding evil as a withdrawal into self-centeredness, Hegel knows this withdrawal as occurring *from the beginning* in the "externalization" and "alienation" of the divine Being, for Absolute Being becomes its own "other," thereby it withdraws into itself and becomes self-centered or "evil." Yet this is that ultimate self-alienation that is consummated in death, in the death of God Himself, and a death that is the death of the abstraction or alienation or "evil" of the divine Being (*Phenomenology of Spirit* 778-780).

That which is simply impossible in all other philosophical thinking, the death or ending of Absolute Being itself, becomes not only possible but necessary in Hegelian thinking, and precisely because this is a genuine dialectical thinking, the only fully dialectical thinking that the West has ever known. And the "evil" that Hegel knows in God is a genuine nothingness, and a fully actual nothingness, one that is the inevitable consequence of an absolute self-negation, an absolute self-negation that is an absolute self-alienation, a self-alienation actually embodying nothingness itself. A traditional apophatic mystical theology can know Godhead itself as an absolute nothingness, but only insofar as it is an absolutely primordial nothingness, Hegelian thinking, on the contrary, knows absolute nothingness as the consequence of an absolute negation or self-negation, and an absolute self-negation occurring in consciousness and history at once. Just as Heidegger is under the deep impact of Hegel in his deconstruction of metaphysics, so, too, is he under that impact in so deeply integrating philosophical and historical thinking. But Heidegger resolutely refuses Hegel's dialectical thinking, and if only thereby is ultimately bound to Being, a bondage to Being that is conceptually ended by Hegel, and ecstatically reversed by Nietzsche.

That reversal is inseparable from Nietzsche's truly new encounter with an absolute nothingness, a nothingness that he could know as a consequence of the death of God, and a nothingness that is an absolutely new chaos, a chaos in which every distinction whatsoever is ended, as a truly new eternal return is now manifest, an eternal return in which identity and difference flow into one another, and nothing at all either preserves its own identity or is different from anything else. This, of course, is the advent of an absolute nihilism, and an absolute nihilism inseparable from an absolute nothingness. Now, existence itself is a pure horror, and one that will be envisioned imaginatively by Nietzsche's successors, who comprehend virtually all of our truly major poets. Yet Nietzsche ever more fully gave himself to an absolute affirmation of this horror, one wholly and ultimately transforming an ancient *amor fati*. Now *amor fati* is an affirmation of the totality of the world just as it is, one with no exceptions or subtractions whatsoever. Even if Nietzsche can call this a Dionysian affirmation (*The Will to Power*, 1041), no such affirmation can be discovered in the ancient world, nor in any world until the advent of Nietzsche. Is it only an absolute nothingness that makes possible such an affirmation, an absolute nothingness in which there is no distinction whatsoever between good and evil, so that an ultimate willing of the good is necessarily an ultimate willing of evil? If Nietzsche is the first thinker to know the uniquely Christian God as a God who ultimately wills an absolute evil, is that the inevitable consequence of the full advent of an absolute nothingness?

No symbol is more distinctively Christian than is the symbol of *felix culpa* or a "fortunate fall," one known by every Christianity knowing a final apocalypse wholly transcending an original paradise, but Nietzsche, too, profoundly enacts a *felix culpa*, which is just why his eternal recurrence is not a primordial eternal return. It is far rather an apocalyptic eternal recurrence, one directed to an absolute future rather than an absolutely primordial past. Nietzsche, in knowing God Himself as the deification of nothingness (*The Antichrist* 18), can even know the absolute No-saying of God as a *felix culpa*, for only the absolute reversal of that No-saying can realize the absolute Yes-saying of Eternal Recurrence, or only the absolute transfiguration of an absolute nothingness can realize apocalypse itself. This very paradigm is a decisive way into our greatest modern art and poetry, and if it is Nietzsche above all who is the philosopher of that poetry and art, it is Nietzsche who in realizing an ultimate horror and nothingness realizes precisely thereby an ultimate joy and affirmation. Now a uniquely Christian *dysangel* truly reverses itself, and if this occurs only by realizing Godhead itself as an absolutely actual absolute nothingness, this can be understood as a necessary and inevitable destiny of that Godhead, a Godhead that *is absolute* sacrifice itself. Hegel and Nietzsche are those philosophers who most profoundly understand an absolute sacrifice, hence they are inevitably philosophers of the Crucified God, but it is Nietzsche who has given us our deepest interior understanding of that sacrifice, and if this is a sacrifice calling forth an absolute nothingness, and one that is fully actual in the depths of our own interior, that interiority is finally exteriority itself, and an absolute exteriority, but only insofar as it is an absolute nothingness.

Is Nietzsche finally only an enemy of God? Or is it Nietzsche alone who can make possible our understanding of the necessity of God's willing an absolute evil, an absolute evil only possible through God, and an absolute evil that Western Christianity has always known in knowing double predestination, wherein the vast majority of humanity is eternally predestined to an eternal Hell. Just as Augustine created the doctrine of predestination, it is Augustine who knows evil and nothingness more deeply than any other pre-modern thinker, and while Augustine will only speak of God's permission of evil, our first philosopher of the will deeply knows the will of God, and knows that will as the ultimate source of every event. Inevitably, it is the will of God that is the sole source of both redemption and damnation, so even if he will not say so, it is an inevitable consequence of Augustinian thinking not only that God wills damnation but that He wills evil, too, and just as He wills damnation in willing redemption, He wills an absolute evil in willing apocalypse itself. In this perspective the Christian God is a true *horror religiosus*, and one reborn not only in Luther and Kierkegaard, but in Nietzsche, too, a Nietzsche who knows that horror more deeply than any other thinker, but that knowledge is finally a liberating knowledge, for thereby and only thereby we can understand the absolute necessity of an absolute evil.

How ironic that Nietzsche in knowing God as the deification of nothingness could know the actuality of God more fully than any other thinker since Hegel. If he knows that actuality as an absolute nothingness, it is nevertheless an absolutely actual absolute nothingness, one making possible Nietzsche's ultimate understanding of an absolute guilt and an absolute *ressentiment*, one only possible by way of an ultimate encounter with that absolute nothingness that is the uniquely Christian God. Thus, if Nietzsche's gospel is the gospel of the death of God, only that death makes possible an actual knowledge of absolute nothingness itself. And this is a knowledge that can only be an actual knowledge by a willing of that absolute nothingness, but that very willing reverses an absolute nothingness, and reverses it by transforming an absolute No-saying into an absolute Yes-saying, a reversal that is the reversal of

Godhead itself, and one only possible through the death of God. Is it Nietzsche who is Luther's purest descendent, the one who has most purely transformed Law into Gospel, or damnation into salvation? And, if Luther's thinking is inseparable from an ultimate *Angst*, and an *Angst* that is truly an encounter with the Nothing, is it Nietzsche who most purely bears that *Angst* in the modern world, an *Angst* apart from which he is no thinker at all?

Is it possible truly to know *Angst* without knowing an absolute nothingness, or to know an absolute nothingness apart from knowing an ultimate *Angst*? Here, a uniquely modern absolute nothingness is a universe removed from a Buddhist absolute nothingness, or from any purely mystical absolute nothingness. Whereas a genuine Buddhism is a pure reversal of any possible nihilism, a truly modern absolute nothingness has inevitably called forth the depths of nihilism, a nihilism simply impossible apart from the full realization of a fully actual absolute nothingness. One is even tempted to say that nothing is more empirically verifiable today than the total presence of an absolute nothingness, an absolute nothingness embodied in our nihilism, and seemingly inescapable therein, or escapable only by the most ultimate leap, a leap that could only be a leap out of the very actuality of our world, or out of the actuality of a postmodern world. Only Nietzsche foresaw postmodernity, or only Nietzsche and Kierkegaard, if only thereby they are truly prophets of our world, but are they prophets enacting absolute reversals of our world, or has such a reversal now become truly impossible? Is an absolute nothingness now so fully embodied that we have no possible perspective apart from it? Is the Nothing thereby silent as the Nothing, so that now we are delivered from any possible *Angst*, and delivered by a truly new anonymity, an anonymity foreclosing any possible individual or interior encounter, thereby not only foreclosing any possibility of the "guilty conscience," but any possibility of an interior encounter with nothingness, or any possibility of an interior awareness of nothingness itself?

A Call

Now it is just a world in which an actual nothingness is all pervasive, that calls to the absolutely primordial have arisen once again, calls reenacting ancient Neoplatonism, and above all so in their calls of ultimate return, and a return from that nothingness that is now engulfing us. Heidegger could be identified as the Plotinus of our world. His is certainly a truly new and comprehensive primordial thinking, and it has had an enormous impact as such, one openly manifest in the radical thinking of Levinas and Derrida, and implicitly present throughout European theology, which for the first time in its history is wholly and comprehensively directed not to the future but to the past. Apparently it is only in America that there are theologians who resist a call to the absolutely primordial, only in America that an apocalyptic horizon is theologically manifest, perhaps because America is the most technological of all nations, and if only thereby the most nihilistic of nations, the one most free of history itself. Nevertheless, Heidegger, unlike his philosophical and theological compatriots, is both an apocalyptic and a primordial thinker, and most apocalyptic insofar as he is a theological thinker, so that if he has given us a truly primordial call, his is nonetheless an apocalyptic call, and most fully so when it is actually heard as a call.

Is it possible for us actually to hear such a call? On the one hand, it is overwhelmingly manifest in religious fundamentalisms throughout the world, but, on the other hand, these are the very movements that are most distant from our new world, and most alien to a genuinely contemporary language, so could it be that the very actuality of our new world is most removed from any possible primordial hearing? Heidegger reached this judgment in his reaction to our technology, but is it possible that the least primordial condition, or that condition most removed from a primordial horizon, is just that condition that generates the deepest longing for the primordial itself? The birth of European Romanticism in its reaction against the Enlightenment generated such a longing, as most fully manifest in Goethe himself,

but this is a truly new epiphany of the primordial, with no real counterparts in the ancient world, so could we say that a realization of a
primordial call in late modernity is also truly new? It surely appears
as such in Heidegger, and less so in Levinas who, despite his attempts
to speak in the language of the Torah, thereby evokes a Torah that is
more primordial than ever before, and more primordial as a purely ahistorical Torah. Of course, every contemporary fundamentalism knows
a purely ahistorical revelation, just as every such fundamentalism is
a movement of eternal return, but is the very call to the primordial
inseparable from a movement of eternal return?

Nothing is more challenging to us than the very possibility of
an ultimate call. Christianity could begin with an ultimate call to
the absolutely new, but has it reached a consummation in which the
absolutely new could only be the absolutely primordial? Are we being
given a new apocalypticism that is a final realization of the absolutely
primordial, thereby realizing the pure orthodoxies of Judaism, Christianity, and Islam alike, and even realizing ancient Oriental vision in
a truly new form? Is this the call that is most powerful in our midst,
and the only call that we can actually hear, or the only ultimate call?
There are postmodern theologies seemingly claiming this, genuinely
radical orthodoxies, but is that the only possible theology in our
world, and the only one that is actually occurring in postmodernity?
Or could this, too, be a deep illusion, an illusion possible only within
an ecclesiastical body, therefore within a truly anti-apocalyptic body?
Within this perspective is it possible to know that a purely primordial
call could only be an absolutely anti-apocalyptic call, or certainly
could only be absolutely anti-apocalyptic for us? Religion itself is now
comprehensively manifest as being a movement of ultimate and eternal
return, and even if this is the very opposite of what we can know as
the deepest Biblical movements, is it a primordial movement alone
that can now be known as an ultimate movement, and has the moment finally arrived when Godhead itself can most comprehensively
be known as primordial Godhead, with no vestiges whatsoever of an
apocalyptic horizon?

If we are now confronting a truly contemporary Either-Or, either the purely primordial or the purely apocalyptic, either an absolute return or an absolutely new apocalyptic movement, it would appear that only the former is possible as a liberating movement, and the latter only possible as a pure nihilism. Moreover, vast numbers of people throughout the world have chosen a purely primordial movement, and if now a new fundamentalism appears to be identical with religion itself, a new conservatism can appear to be identical with politics itself, and each can identify their real or ultimate opponent as some form of nihilism, a nihilism now seemingly inevitable in every non-primordial movement and every non-primordial call. Thus the advent of a truly new and comprehensive primordial call is transforming every other call into a nihilistic call, and that which is the true opposite of a primordial call, the call of apocalypse itself, is now seemingly manifest as a purely nihilistic call, and if this is a renewal and reenactment of an originally Christian transformation of the apocalyptic into the primordial, now it occurs within a universal horizon, thereby occurring as a comprehensive negation of every possible apocalyptic ground. Hence a call can now be heard, and overwhelmingly heard, which is not only a call to the absolutely primordial, but that transforms every other ultimate call into either a purely empty or a purely nihilistic call.

Despite all appearances to the contrary, is it possible that a purely orthodox theology is truly engaging our world, may indeed be its clearest voice, a voice speaking the primordial and the primordial alone? And even if this is a truly new primordial epiphany, does it truly renew the purely primordial ground of all orthodox theology, but only now within the horizon of the world itself? How ironic this would be within a Heidegerrian perspective, for no philosopher has been more purely anti-orthodox than Heidegger, and yet no philosopher since Plotinus has so profoundly called forth the purely primordial; indeed, it is all too clear that Heidegger's thinking precisely as a primordial thinking is by necessity an anti-orthodox theological thinking, as most manifest in either his refusal to think "God" or his assaults upon the Christian God in *Beiträge*. Heidegger's is the richest and most powerful philosophical language of our century, but the language of a contemporary orthodox theology is the very opposite, only becoming alive in assaults upon its enemies, and never being able to evoke Christian dogma itself in anything but an empty language, an empty language that is a truly passive language, and one both reflecting and engaging the deep passivity of its hearers. But is that passivity at bottom the universal condition of a postmodern world, so that the truly passive language of a new theological orthodoxy does actually engage our world, and not only engages it, but ultimately sanctions our new primordial movements, thus making possible a new peace and serenity even in the presence of a totally technological or totally objectified world?

Perhaps we have now transcended any possible Either-Or, and transcended it by our radically new ability to hear nothing but a primordial call. If a new technological world is now becoming all in all, is that a dissolution of every interior hearing that is not a hearing of the primordial itself, thus making possible for the first time a universal hearing of primordial Godhead, and the universal call of eternal return? And just as the deepest mystics can know primordial Godhead as an absolute nothingness, is our new world a reflection of such a nothingness, but now one embodied historically as it never was before, and ever more fully embodied historically in a new and universal process of absolute objectification? Does not that very process end every ultimate or interior call that is not an absolutely primordial call, or does it make possible a new and even more ultimate reversal of every primordial call, one in genuine continuity with Biblical apocalypticism, and with Christianity's own original ground? Is it possible that the very universality of a new primordial call could make possible such a reversal; do we hear a call to that reversal in hearing a truly new emptiness and passivity; does that very emptiness impel us to its reversal, a reversal apart from which we could only be passive and empty? Of course, it is possible to meet this situation with a new dissolution or a new suspension of every possible ultimate call, one that occurs in a purely academic analytic philosophy, if not in a new academic world as a whole, but is not such a suspension itself a deep witness to the very passivity of our new world?

While it is true that such a passivity does truly numb a primordial call that otherwise would be overwhelming, and thus actually is a source of sanity and order, is it not nevertheless necessary that we become open to a call that is the very opposite of a primordial call, never forgetting that Heidegger employed a primordial call in sanctioning Nazism, for a primordial call can become a truly demonic or Satanic call, and above all so in a fully modern or postmodern world. The Hebrew prophets could know a primordial call as a truly idolatrous or demonic call, but only in the face of that call to eternal return did they proclaim and enact an ultimate transformation, and a transformation truly inverting every possible eternal return, which is inevitable in a genuinely apocalyptic movement. Hence a prophetic call, or the prophetic call of the Bible, is a genuinely apocalyptic call, and as such it is a pure reversal of every possible primordial call, and is so by calling forth that absolute future that is a reversal of every possible past. Is it possible for us to hear the call of such a future, not a future that is an enlargement or perpetuation of our world, but one that is its very reversal, and not its reversal by way of a primordial movement, but its reversal by way of an apocalyptic movement, an apocalyptic movement truly turning the world upside down?

Primordial movements are inevitably deeply conservative or reactionary movements, whereas genuinely or fully apocalyptic movements are inevitably revolutionary, and all of the great revolutionary political movements of the modern world share a deeply apocalyptic ground. Even the scientific revolution of the seventeenth century can be understood as an apocalyptic movement, one truly bringing an end to an old world or an old totality and ushering in an absolutely new world. Both political revolution and the scientific revolution were profound threats to the established Church, so much so that they ultimately reduced the Church to a sectarian body or bodies, and just as ancient apocalypticism could know all established religion and law as the very body of the Antichrist, a truly modern apocalypticism knows all established religion as its purest enemy. Yet modern apocalypticism is truly universal in its scope as ancient apocalypticism was not, an apocalypticism comprehending the worlds of art, thinking, and politics, and giving us our most comprehensive thinking and vision. Has all such apocalypticism simply vanished? Or has it become its own opposite, is it now manifest and real only as an absolutely primordial movement, and is an apocalyptic call now only hearable as a primordial call?

Heidegger's conjunction of the primordial and the apocalyptic is not unique. It is echoed in Derrida even if not in Levinas; indeed, *Finnegans Wake* is profoundly primordial and profoundly apocalyptic at once, and if the *Wake* is our fullest contemporary epic, is that an epic calling us to an ultimately primordial movement that is an ultimately apocalyptic movement? Nothing is more powerful in the *Wake* than is a pure and total call, but it is a total call only by being both a totally primordial and a totally apocalyptic call, a call embodied both in the primordial body of "Here Comes Everybody" and the apocalyptic body of Anna Livia Plurabelle, yet the concluding apocalypse of this ultimate epic is a total transfiguration of the primordial body of H.C.E. into the apocalyptic body of A.L.P. Thereby the absolutely primordial resolution of *Faust* is truly reversed, and with that reversal there occurs an ending of every truly primordial ground, or the ending of every truly primordial ground that is not an apocalyptic ground. Inevitably, this is a total transformation of the primordial itself, and thereafter the truly or purely primordial can only be envisioned as an absolute negativity, an envisionment already occurring in a Melville or a Kafka, but one that occurs most purely in Beckett, that true son of Joyce who could know the *Wake* as being purgatorial in the absolute absence of the Absolute. Is it possible that a purely primordial voice could now be actual only as an absolutely negative voice, or a purely primordial call now only fully real as a purely negative call, one that we can actually hear only in our most passive moments, or only in a fully inactual condition? This alone could account for the power of a primordial call in a truly postmodern world, a call that Blake could know as the call of Satan, and Nietzsche could know as the call of the uniquely Christian God.

Both the purely primordial and the purely apocalyptic can each be known as an absolute nothingness, and neither the purely primordial nor the purely apocalyptic can escape or transcend that horizon; each is manifest as a pathological fantasy in our common thinking and judgment, and yet their profound power in our history is undeniable. If ours is a unique historical moment and world, perhaps it is so most clearly in calling us to a truly new world, an absolutely new world never fully manifest historically before, one demanding an absolute transfiguration, a transfiguration inseparable from that new world. Israel underwent such a transfiguration as a consequence of the first exile, an exile in which Israel lost every ground of its pre-exilic life, but an exile making possible an ultimate transformation of Israel. Are we, too, undergoing an ultimate exile, an exile from that interiority that is most distinctive of a post-Classical Western world, an interiority inseparable from that conscience, consciousness, and existence that we once knew, but an interiority now becoming the very opposite of itself, and doing so in the very advent of a new and total exteriority? That exteriority surely parallels that ultimate exile undergone by ancient Israel, but this made possible for Israel a rebirth that was the birth of a new and ultimate world, a radically new world of faith fully enacted both in the Book of Job and in Second Isaiah, and a faith wholly liberated from every ground in an ancient or archaic world, and one making possible an absolutely new life.

Simply to become aware of the immense distance between pre-exilic and post-exilic Israel is to become aware of the possibility of an ultimate historical transformation. If it is just such a transformation to which we are now being called, one that indeed is embodied in our very midst, a movement of ultimate or eternal return could only be a refusal of this challenge, and a refusal inseparable from an ultimate passivity. Both Heidegger and Levinas have enacted a call to a pure and total passivity, and a genuine even if empty passivity is embodied throughout the world of postmodernity. But is that passivity a veil that we must break through, and break through with an ultimate act of affirmation? While such an act is seemingly impossible in our new world, it is not impossible if our deepest depths are undergoing an ultimate transformation. And if those depths are ultimately the depths of Godhead itself, and of a Godhead undergoing an absolute transfiguration, that transfiguration could only be absolute act itself. Such a transfiguration would have an ultimate effect upon our history, and upon our interiority as well, and even if that is a purely negative effect, and one realizing itself in a purely negative mode, it would nonetheless be an absolute transfiguration. That is a transfiguration that Christianity has always most deeply known, and even if a uniquely Christian repression has truly repressed or hidden that transfiguration, it has nevertheless occurred, as witness that ultimate transformation of Christianity that has indeed occurred.

Could such a transformation be occurring even now, and is this the transformation to which we are now called, indeed, a transformation even now occurring within and about us? Even if that transformation can actually appear as a dark and empty one, could its very darkness be a way for us to an ultimate light? A primal call occurring throughout our history is a call to a descent into the deepest darkness, and this call has become ever more universal in the late modern world, perhaps reaching a consummation with the advent of postmodernity. If so, this is a call that we can resist but cannot evade, and if we accept it and make it our own, we thereby become open to the possibility of transfiguration, a transfiguration not our own but one given us by depths wholly beyond ourselves, and beyond ourselves in the depths of Godhead itself. If that Godhead is even now undergoing an absolute transfiguration, it is wholly other than any possible primordial Godhead, just as it is beyond everything that we have known as God. Hence it is inseparable from the death or dissolution or self-emptying of primordial Godhead, a death of God that we can know as an absolute liberation, an absolute liberation making possible an absolute apocalypse. Can we greet that apocalypse with an ultimate affirmation, an ultimate affirmation releasing an ultimate joy, and is this to ask if it is possible for even us to say Yes, and to say Yes with a full and ultimate assurance? Certainly this would be an affirmation of the absolutely new, but an epiphany of the absolutely new inseparable from an epiphany of an absolute darkness, a darkness that we must finally embody and affirm if we are to become open to *absolute novum*. Only then can we truly say Yes, and say Yes to that darkness if only to make possible an absolute Yes.

Yes, we are the primordial body of Here Comes Everybody, but we are being called to the apocalyptic body of Anna Livia Plurabelle, an apocalyptic A.L.P. that Dante could know as Beatrice, and Blake could know as Jerusalem, but that apocalyptic body is possible only by way of the absolute transfiguration of that primordial body that is H.C.E., a transfiguration that is finally the transfiguration of an absolute negativity. That transfiguration can only occur as a consequence of the full epiphany of an ultimate negativity, and a truly comprehensive and universal negativity, one that certainly can be known in postmodernity, and certainly known in our new and empty interiors. Yet only a deep and ultimate emptiness is open to an ultimate transfiguration, this primal truth is known not only by every higher mysticism but by every deeper expression of the imagination, just as it is known by the Christian in knowing the Crucifixion as being absolutely essential to apocalypse, and thus knowing the death of God as being essential to the apocalypse of the Godhead. If that apocalypse is occurring even now, it could do so only in a dark and empty mode, but that is a darkness that is finally light, a Satan that is finally Jerusalem. Is it Jerusalem who is now most deeply calling us, and even if that could occur only through the darkness of Satan, or the darkness of a total nihilism, can we nonetheless greet that calling with an ultimate affirmation and an ecstatic joy?

Index

Made in the USA
Lexington, KY
27 August 2015